Something
To
Think
About

Perumal Krishnan

PublishAmerica
Baltimore

First printing

ISBN: 1-4137-4795-7
PUBLISHED BY PUBLISHAMERICA, LLLP
www.publishamerica.com
Baltimore

Printed in the United States of America

DEDICATED
TO
ALL THOSE KILLED AND WOUNDED
AND
WAITING TO BE KILLED AND WOUNDED
IN IRAQ
BECAUSE OF THE RECENT
INVASION AND OCCUPATION
FOR
OIL AND GLOBAL DOMINATION

Table of Contents

Introduction

Hello, there! At the outset, let me thank each and everyone of you for giving me this opportunity to share my views and thoughts with you.

My name is Perumal Krishnan. I was born and brought up in India, where I earned a Master's degree in Engineering. After working for a while in India, I moved to England to pursue my research for a Ph.D. While writing my thesis, for multifarious personal reasons, I decided to seek employment and settle down in England. I am an engineer, and most of my working life I have been developing a lot of computer application software for scientific, engineering, and commercial applications. I am blessed with 3 wonderful women, viz. my wife and two daughters. I have lived and worked in various cities in India, England, Saudi Arabia, Germany and the USA. Besides, as tourists along with my family, I have visited various cities in India, the United Kingdom, Europe, Greece, Egypt, Malaysia, Singapore, Thailand, the USA and Canada. As such, I have been really very fortunate to meet with people from various parts of the world and witness their varied culture and way of living. I recall herein my personal experiences, beliefs, and philosophy about life. I intend to document, in this book, my thoughts and views on what is going on with our lives now, and what we can do to live well and let others live well with us.

As I very much want the readers to read and think over the contents of this book, I decided on the title, *Something To Think About*. Please pause for a moment to consider this. Unless you were otherwise forced to because of circumstances beyond your control, invariably you are what your thoughts have made you to be. Do you get what I mean? Say, you are a teacher now. You got there mainly because this is what you wanted to be in the first instance and then pursued it further to get there. So, my point is, we must weigh and be vigilant of what we think first, and then follow it up further in line with what we decide. What happens when we make hasty decisions? "Do it in haste and repent at leisure." We get the same result when we do not promptly do whatever we need to do as well. We mould our way of life based on what we think first, and hence the real need to be careful in what we think.

This book is meant for everyone, irrespective of where we live, or what we do and believe in our day-to-day life. Please don't rush to read this book in a hurry. This is not a novel. This book is about you, your family, your community, and your country. You may not be shrewd and smart. But, at the same time, you don't have to be naive and blind to believe everything you hear from others, in particular the politicians. Take your time to read this book and then spare some time to relax and think it through calmly, clearly and carefully on what you read. Please do not prejudge the presented views with any preconceived notion, or personal bias or prejudice. Think over the details with an open mind. Chances are you may not agree with my views and suggestions. Of course, you are entitled to your opinion, just as I am entitled to mine, and I respect you for the same. But, if any of my views and suggestions make sense and appear to be acceptable to you, then act accordingly instead of just doing nothing. This is because I don't want you to repent at leisure by doing nothing. If we think through clearly, make positive moves to guide and control our own destiny and pursue them further with persistence, then our living conditions will improve. Don't rely and wait on others to do it for you because, the fact is, they won't. This is your life. Who is better equipped than you to take care of it? Please, use your conscience and common sense to arrive at a positive and practical decision, and then to act on it accordingly.

You may be a hardcore extremist with your political persuasion or a fundamentalist in your religious beliefs or, like most us, just an ordinary citizen working really hard to make a decent living, and as such, either have no time or can't be really bothered to give serious considerations to what is going on around you and the world at large. The first two types of people can cause great concern or even chaos to a community because of their extremist left or right wing views. But, in a country where the democracy still seems to exist, at least in theory, it is the third category known as the "swing voters" who decide the fate of that country. It is sad to note that this third category does not realize the power they have in a democratic set up, nor is it taking advantage of that power to ensure better and safer living conditions.

A perusal of the topics briefed below and covered in detail later in the subsequent chapters will show that most of the presented material is meant for everyone. However, my main focus is on the "swing voters." It is time this category realizes that they cannot afford to rely on the corrupt lawmakers to look after the people's interests. If the people wake up, at least now, and fight for their rights in a peaceful way, then they have a real chance to keep the vested interests and politicians well under control. This will enable us ALL to ensure a safe, secure and prosperous society, not just for a set of privileged few who are shrewd and smart in "screwing" innocent, poor, weak and vulnerable people.

What I honestly want to impress upon the readers is just this. Don't trust anyone, especially the politicians and their rhetoric. Nobody, but you and your family, is going to care about you and your happiness. You need to be smart to take care of yourself and your family. You should not blindly believe everything the politicians and vested interests say with their rhetoric on patriotism, national security, war on terror, etc., etc.

What really amazes me is this. Almost all the time, the politicians continue to say packs of lies, like what Mr. Bush and Mr. Blair are doing, just to fool the people whom they are supposed to protect and serve. Then, they go to the church to pray. Do they really believe in God, or is it just another photo opportunity? Are they begging for God's forgiveness for all the sins they committed? Do they have any real conscience to think for a moment the countless number of causalities they caused, and continue to cause unnecessarily in Iraq; about the consequent impact on the families of those killed or wounded, national economy and our ever-increasing national debt?

Please listen to what the politicians say. But, use your head to reason out their motive behind. At the same time, listen to the arguments put forward by the opposition as well. Don't take anybody and anything for granted. Ask them to explain how ordinary hard working people like you are likely to benefit by whatever they are preaching. Ask them to tell you how it is going to help the poor, weak and vulnerable. Let them explain how it is going to help those who are unable to help themselves. But, after you listen to both sides, the most important thing you owe it to yourself and to your country is to use your head clearly and calmly to decide, like a jury, on what you think should be the correct course of action. Don't just believe what the politicians preach and promise. Refuse to let them use you to get what they want. Be smart and vigilant. To put it bluntly, don't let them continue to "screw" you.

As for me, I am just another ordinary citizen, like most of you. I don't pretend, or intend, to be an expert on politics, religion, or the cultural and social behaviour of the human being. Even though I lived and worked in various countries, in the recent years, I have been mostly living in the USA and the UK. As such, most of the details being dealt with in this book as regards to the current affairs will relate to the present and past political affairs of these two countries, mainly America. I don't have any personal bias or persuasion towards any political party. To be honest, I do NOT have any regard or respect for ANY politician. In my opinion, the politicians are nothing but the puppets of the vested interests such as trade unions, National Rifle Association, drug manufacturers, insurance companies, big corporations, etc., etc. who make generous campaign contributions to these politicians. Please think it through. Why do you think these vested interests pay so much of money to these politicians? Is it because they just love them and want to help them? Give me a break. Prior to the election, these politicians give all sorts of promises to get your votes. Once the election is over, then that is it. You won't see them again until the next election. In return for the received campaign contributions, these politicians are kept under constant pressure to work for the lobbying groups to take care of their vested interests, not your interests, even though it is you who elected them and it is you who pay their salary out of your hard earned tax money.

As per one of the reports dated February 24, 2002 by Bernie Sanders, http://bernie.house.gov/documents/opeds/20020214185510.asp,
"The drug companies have 600-plus paid lobbyists on Capitol Hill, more than one lobbyist for each Member of the House and Senate. Some of their lead lobbyists are former Congressional leaders of the Republican and Democratic parties."

Can you believe it? It has been reported that most of the laws, including the latest Medicare Prescription Drug Law, are drafted by the lobbyists, but not by your elected candidates whose only job is to make the law, with your consent, to take care of your interests. Besides, as revealed in the latest documentary film, *Fahrenheit 9/11*, by Michael Moore, most of the lawmakers don't really check the details of the law that they are voting for. Unfortunately, the *Patriot Act* is just another solid example in this context, I am afraid.

In case you haven't realized yet, who do you think is eventually paying for:

- The huge profits these vested interests make,
- The cost towards the campaign contributions,
- The cost towards media advertisements, and
- The substantial salary for each and every one of their lobbyists?

Every time we buy their product and/or use their services, eventually it is YOU and I who pay towards all these. Can you just imagine how much the cost of the products and services will get cut down, if we pay towards just the manufacturing and service related expenses plus a reasonable limited advertisements and profit? Don't you think we can't afford to let the corrupted status quo continue?

There are numerous sources available to monitor the behaviour of the lobbyists. Check out *http://www.opensecrets.org/about/index.asp*. This website for *The Center for Responsive Politics* is a non-partisan, non-profit research group based in Washington, D.C. that tracks money in politics, and its effect on elections and public policy. The Center conducts computer-based research on campaign finance issues for the news media, academics, activists, and the public at large. The Center's work is aimed at creating a more educated voter, an involved citizenry, and a more responsive government.

However, at the same time unfortunately, we have to be aware of what the reality is now in respect of the present political system. With this in mind, under the circumstances, we have no other alternative but to make a carefully considered choice for the lesser of the two evils.

As I have been a computer software developer most of my life, I sincerely try to look at each situation logically the way it is practised, ***not preached***, and then attempt to analyse its impact on our day-to-day life. Wherever it is appropriate, I put forward my views on how we can arrive at a possible corrective course of action that will hopefully lead to some fairness and happiness to **ALL**. This is for your valuable consideration. Please think it over carefully with an open mind and then decide on whatever you think is appropriate and right for your particular case. Let your own conscience and common sense, but not any prejudice or jealousy, be the guiding tool in arriving at a decision. It is your life and your happiness we are talking about. It is up to you to take control of your own destiny. Remember the saying, "you can take a horse to water, but you cannot make it drink." If you are happy to let the current chaos and status quo continue, it is up to you. But, if you really want to get better yourself, then please do something positive towards it.

Please find below brief overviews of the topics that relate to us either directly or indirectly in our day-to-day lives. While I present the facts, as I see them, and discuss various issues in each topic that concern us, I ask pertinent questions followed by my views on what I consider to be the relevant and right approach to resolve the issues.

I list, as a summary, some ***Points for 'Something To Think About'*** at the end of each chapter, for your ready reference. Besides, wherever it is appropriate and relevant, I also provide the essential section of the source material that I would very much like you to check out.

Once again, I plead with you to please weigh what I say and act in line with what you may decide. We all have a tendency to take credit when things work out right. But, when things go wrong, we always tend to blame it on others, as if we have no part in it. We don't like to take responsibility for our action or inaction. Unless, and until, you take full responsibility to take control of your own destiny by getting your priorities right and doing the right things, in the right peaceful way, at the right time, you have to realize that the current chaos will continue forever. In this context, please remind yourself all the time of this fact. Success comes to only those who get their priorities right and act on them accordingly. Besides, you have to also realize that you get what you pay for.

Democracy and Lawmakers: Do the lawmakers really care about your welfare, especially of those who are poor, weak, and vulnerable and those who cannot help themselves? According to the definition of democracy, **the government must be of the people, by the people, and for the people.** Is that what you see now? How can you force the lawmakers to work for you and not for the vested interests? How can you monitor the behaviour and day-to-day activities of the lawmakers? Lawmakers are there because you hired and sent them there, and you are paying their salary out of your tax money. As such, how can you make them report to you on a regular basis on everything they do, or don't?

War on Terror: We hear so much about war on terror worldwide. Who are these terrorists and why are they inflicting this terror? Why is nothing positive and effective done in respect of the terror from the domestic thugs, robbers, rapists and gangsters? As for the foreign terrorists, why are they hell bent on attacking only American and Israeli interests and those governments that are bullied into supporting America? Did Iraq pose any real threat to America prior to the recent invasion? What is the real reason for America to invade and occupy Iraq? Why is almost the entire world population opposed to the recent invasion, while they supported the previous Gulf War and the effort to eliminate the evil activities of Osama bin Laden? Why doesn't America let the United Nations do its job effectively? Is America really a super power in respect of resolving the issues in a civilized way? The right wing leaders of both America and Israel have a few things in common viz. arrogance and indifference to the world opinions. Their attitude is "I have the mighty military. I can do what I like, when I like and how I like. You dare to stop me?" Is this a civilized approach toward resolving international problems?

Violence: We all hate violence, especially when it hits us personally. Violence breeds violence. But, what are we doing to contain it? How do we react and respond to violence that we see in sports, movies, and real life? Do we really need violence as part of our entertainment? Why should any decent civilian need any gun at home?

Media: Media is the most powerful means for communication, education, and entertainment. As such, it can make or break the true image of a person, or a society, or a country. Do we really get a fair presentation of the facts? No! Why not? What can you do to force the media to compile and convey correct information and not fabricated presentation in line with the vested interests of the owners of the media?

Marriage and Family life: We are all part of a big or a small family. A person's character is cultivated and controlled at home first and then modified in the society where that person lives. So, in the interest of everyone in a society, it is essential that we ensure a loving and caring, happily married family life. Children out of a broken family invariably end up not reaching their true potential because of the unsecured feelings. Have you got a happy marriage and family life? How stable is your marriage? How can we work towards a happy married life? What sort of family life do you lead? Are you like a role model to your children? No! Why not? What possibly can you try and do to be a real good role model? How loving, caring and considerate are you towards your family, neighbours and your community? Let us check it out.

Race and Religion: Do we have a good race relationship between various people? We may have variations with our features, characters, and skin colors, but since we are all God's children, we all belong to just one race: the human race. This classification of whites, blacks, etc. is a man made evil, set up to segregate God's children based on the skin color. Even in our own family, we are different, may not agree on everything, and may argue a lot. But, we don't fight and kill each other on this count. We agree to disagree, and learn to live together as one family. Why can't we extend this approach beyond our family to our community, country, and then other countries as well? Should we have Affirmative Action in the fields of education and employment **for some more time?** As for religion, what really matters is how it is practiced, and not how it is preached. The basic principle of any religion must be to love and care for each other. Extremists on either side of race and religion issues instigate and induce violence between people to satisfy their vested agenda. Why is there so much hatred and violence within various sects of any religion? We should not blindly believe preaching or rituals of any religion. We must use our head and common sense. Respect others for their belief and faith in their religion, just as you would have others do towards you. Live and let live. Don't insist and impose your views and beliefs on others. What is the real status of women in our society? Do women really have equal rights? Do we really respect the people of other races and religions? What makes you think that your race and religion are better than those of others? What can we do to improve the race relationship in our community? What can we do to educate people to respect other races and religions?

Working for Living: Irrespective of whatever you may do for your living, I take it that you really sweat hard to make profit to your employer and shareholders. In return, do you get well-deserved respect and share of the profit? Do you have a caring working environment? Are you allowed to participate in the policy making process of your work place? No! Why not?

What can you do to improve the working conditions for every one in your work place? How good are the working conditions for the women? Are you fully aware of all the dirty tricks of the big corporations that avoid paying due taxes to our governments? What can you do to enforce laws that will prevent these corporations from controlling your government and from taking your jobs offshore to places like China, India, Mexico, etc.? How can you eradicate the pillars, bricks and bones of these big corrupt corporations? The answer is simple.

Let us cover these topics in detail in the following chapters. Please do make a sincere, serious and persistent effort to do the right things at all times, and then stand up and fight peacefully for your right to lead happy, prosperous and peaceful life. I believe in the concept of "Do the best you can and leave the rest to God." Good Luck, and God bless.

Points for *Something To Think About*:

- You are what your thoughts have made you to be. So, take care of what you think.
- Do it in haste and repent at leisure.
- Use your conscience and common sense to think calmly, clearly and carefully to decide on positive moves to guide and control your destiny.
- Fight for your rights in a peaceful way.
- Don't take anyone or anything, especially the politicians and their rhetoric, for granted. Listen, but weigh what they say.
- Politicians are nothing but the puppets of the vested interests.
- Be critical and careful in electing the lesser of the two evils.
- You can take a horse to water, but you cannot make it drink.
- Success comes to only those who get their priorities right and pursue them persistently.
- Take responsibility for every one of your actions as well as inactions.
- Do the best you can and leave the rest to God.

Democracy and Lawmakers

What is the definition for democracy?

The American's Creed, *http://www.usflag.org/american.creed.html*, accepted as of April 3, 1918 states as follows:
"I believe in the United States of America as a Government of the people, by the people, for the people, whose just powers are derived from the consent of the governed; a democracy in a Republic; a sovereign Nation of many sovereign States; a perfect Union, one and inseparable; established upon those principles of freedom, equality, justice, and humanity for which American patriots sacrificed their lives and fortunes.
I therefore believe it is my duty to my Country to love it; to support its Constitution; to obey its laws; to respect its flag, and to defend it against all enemies."

The INS document M-76 of the U.S. Department of Justice viz. *A Welcome to U.S.A. Citizenship,* lists

1. "The Duties of a Citizen,"
2. "Rights and Privileges of a Citizen," and
3. "The Five Qualities of the Good Citizen"

As a citizen, we must be aware of these duties, rights and privileges and hence the contents under these three headings are presented, as a ready reference, at the end of this chapter.

If we want our democracy to function properly, I believe that every citizen must be aware of our rights and responsibilities. Because of the relevance to this topic, the following right and two duties, listed at the end of this chapter, will be referred to often:

  • *I have the right to vote. By my vote I choose the public officers who are really my servants.*
  • *It is my duty to vote, so my government may truly represent the will of*

the people.
   • *It is my duty, by my votes and my influence, to correct injustice.*

So, as per the American's Creed, the American citizen believes in America as the people's government, administered by the people's elected candidates, to take care of the people's interests with the people's consent.

Yes, this is as defined for the American political system. But, no doubt, this definition of democracy viz. **the government of the people, by the people and for the people**, is appropriate and applicable to every democratic country. As per this definition, each and every one of YOU, the people, own your government. YOU select and elect somebody of your choice as your representative to run the day-to-day administration of YOUR government. Everyone, starting from the President or the Prime Minister, working for YOUR government is nothing but your employee and servant. The one and only duty of these elected employees is to protect and take real good care of you and your interests **with your consent.** This is with a view to ensure freedom, equality, justice and humanity to everyone. This is how the set up is for a democracy. Let us explore this in detail, a bit later, to find out how this is really functioning.

Okay, it sounds really great and wonderful. You, the citizens but not any crazy creature like Saddam Hussein, have the power to control your destiny. It must be remembered, it is a big responsibility bestowed on every citizen of a democratic country.

As for the American citizens, the responsibilities are far greater than those of the citizens of other nations purely because, whether anyone likes it or not, America is the only super power in this planet now because it has the most powerful military. This reality has its far-reaching implications on ensuring peace, freedom, prosperity, equality, justice and humanity to the citizens of other countries as well. So, in the interest of the well being of everyone in this planet, American citizens must be critical and careful in carrying out their responsibilities in respect of electing their candidates, top to bottom, in all levels, viz. local, state and federal levels with a very special emphasis on the federal level.

As a citizen you are obliged to perform certain duties in return for certain rights and privileges you are blessed with. The most important duty, in line with the relevant right the people have, is to **vote for a candidate of their choice, so that their government truly represents the will of the people**. Let us checkout whether in reality your government is of the people, by the people, and for the people. In case any of you, the American citizens, are not aware of the constitutional set up of your government, please note that the American Government consists of three branches: Legislative Branch, Executive Branch and Judiciary Branch.

Government of the people.

Thank God, this principle is still holding true. You, the citizens, still own your government. A formal and declared dictator is not controlling the country yet. As such, you collectively have the power to control your own destiny and that of your country. But, the main concern that I have here is, you the citizens don't realize this enormous power you have and use it in the best interests of everyone around you.

Government by the people.

Your **ELECTED** employees must administer your government so that it truly represents the will of the people. Let us examine to find out whether your employees are really elected by all the people or not.

The Legislative Branch is the Congress and it consists of the Senate and the House of Representatives. The people have the full responsibility to elect the members of the Congress through their most powerful votes. In the absence of any published report to the contrary, it seems certain that the people elect their members of the congress. This is good news.

The Executive Branch consists of the President, the Vice President and the Members of the Cabinet who advise the President. I am sure that the founding fathers of the American Constitution must have had some real justifiable reasons as to **why the President needs to be elected <u>purely</u> by the electoral votes, but NOT by the popular votes of the people**. As for me, I am yet to be convinced of the justification behind this set up.

According to me it is a very big mistake, as witnessed in the year 2000

Presidential election, since it does not truly represent the will of all the people. Anyway, whether it is right or wrong, this is what we have now, according to the Constitution of the USA. The President of the USA being the most powerful person on this planet, it is extremely important that we have a very sound and just system where your President is **elected** by the popular votes of the people, but definitely **not indirectly selected** by the politically nominated and motivated Supreme Court Judges. If we fail to realize and rectify this serious flaw in the present system, then the entire world will continue to be in chaos like how it is right now. All I can think of is that an appropriate Constitutional amendment is the only solution to resolve this serious issue. But, whether it will really happen or not is anybody's guess.

The entire world was laughing at the American democracy when they witnessed what happened in Florida in the year 2000 Presidential election. Let us examine a bit on what was going on here.

As per website: http://www.archives.gov/federal_register/ electoral_college/popular_vote_2000.html

Mr. Bush got 50,456,062 (Florida votes 2,912,790) popular votes and Mr. Gore got 50,996,582 (Florida votes 2,912,253) popular votes. In line with the definition of the democracy, your President must be the one as decided by the votes of **ALL** the people, viz. popular votes. On this basis Mr. Gore should have won the election since he had 540,520 more votes than Mr. Bush. Please checkout the Florida votes. Mr. Gore lost just by 537 popular votes in Florida in spite of all the fraud activities carried out by Katherine Harris and Governor Jebb Bush.

As per the website: *http://www.archives.gov/federal_register/ electoral_college/votes_2000.html*

Mr. Bush got 271 electoral votes and Mr. Gore got 266 electoral votes. As per the constitution, the President must be elected by the electoral votes, **but not by the popular votes**. As such, Mr. Bush was declared as the winner by just 5 electoral votes.

Now let us see what was going on by way of fraud activities in Florida during the year 2000 Presidential Election. In this context, another sad and unfortunate reality is, if we want to know the facts on what is going on here within the US governments, we have to find that out from the media of other countries like Europe. We cannot trust any USA media to give us the facts on what is really going on in the USA. There is nothing wrong with the journalists. They are extremely sharp, smart and shrewd in collecting the facts. But, it is the program producers, controlled by the media owners, who decide on what, when, where and how, we the public, should be kept informed.

With a view to gather information on what happened in Florida election, I entered the keywords "Florida Election year 2000" for the internet search engine and I got 732,000 links providing all sorts of the details in some form or other on the disgraceful election fraud by the administration of the Florida Governor Bush. Obviously, we cannot go through each and every one of these sources. The best source for real consolidated information in this respect, in my opinion, is the 1ˢᵗ chapter in the book *Stupid White Men*, one of the worldwide #1 best sellers. The author, Mr. Michael Moore, had done an excellent job to educate the people by exposing the evils of Florida administration. Of course, he had listed all the relevant sources to back up the information.

Besides, checkout the following sources also as they are real good eye openers:
http://www.ericblumrich.com/gta.html
http://www.us-democratorship.com/links.htm
http://www.gregpalast.com/detail.cfm?artid=29&row=1
http://www.thenation.com/docprint.mhtml?i=20010205&s=palast
http://www.thenation.com/docprint.mhtml?i=20010430&s=lantigua
http://www.usccr.gov/

Let us collect some summarized salient information from these sources on how the injustice was inflicted on not only the citizens of Florida, but everyone on this planet.

Florida Governor Bush, as we all know, is the brother of George W. Bush. On top of this, Katherine Harris was the Florida's Secretary of State in charge of the elections in Florida **AND** Head of the Bush election campaign in Florida. Don't you see the conflict of interest here? How can you expect any fairness then? Anyway, let us continue.

It is a well-established fact that most of the poor and low income group of people like Afro Americans and Hispanic population prefer to vote for the Democrats hoping that their grievances will be well addressed by the Democrats better than the Republicans. So, what can the Governor Bush do to help his brother win the election? Well in advance as preparation for the ensuing election in 2000, the Republican controlled State legislature made a law in 1998 to the effect that ex-felons cannot vote in Florida. This means that 31 % of all black men in Florida are prohibited from voting. Good. They are making progress in getting rid of unwanted elements that will most likely vote for Democrats. But, will that be enough? May be not. So, in 1999, Katherine Harris paid $4 million to a private software company, DBT, with strong ties to the Republican party, to get a list that will eliminate all the ex-felons, the people who had similar names, same date of birth and similar Social Security Numbers as the ex-felons, from the eligible voters list. As desired and dictated by Katherine Harris, the DBT got rid of around 173,000 registered voters. Besides, just to play it safe, an additional 8,000 voters were also taken off the eligible voters list because the DBT used a false list on the former convicted felons. This list was supplied by the State of Texas whose Governor was George W. Bush at that time.

Please note that Mr. Bush won Florida by 537 popular votes and 5 electoral votes, after getting rid of thousands of registered voters in Florida. What happens to our basic belief: "all men are created equal" and "every vote counts"? I leave it to you to make your own judgement. No wonder, the entire world was laughing at the American Democracy since it was stinking in Florida. What did US media do? NOTHING. British reporters dug deep into this episode to expose these evil acts in Florida. I echo herein, what Michael Moore says, "It is a sad day when we have to look to a country 5,000 miles away to find out the truth about our own elections." US media picks up the story later. Is it that US media have no adequate resources and technologies to inform the people first? Getting the facts is just the initial step. But, as briefed before, the media owners control the presentation of the facts. Who owns the US media? Yes, you guessed it right. It is owned and controlled by none other than the real big rich corporations with close ties to the right wing political persuasion. We will explore this aspect a bit later in the "Media" chapter.

We can go on forever on this subject, and this Florida election episode could contribute quite a lot for numerous books. I would like to move on after providing some essential excerpts from a few sources. As per the website: *http://www.thenation.com/docprint.mhtml?i=20010430&s=lantigua*

"Florida state elections officials, and hired data crunchers, used computers to target thousands of voters, many of whom were then purged from the voter rolls without reason. And many thousands more saw their votes thrown out as a result of error-prone voting machines, and poorly designed ballots, the results of an underfunded and chaotic electoral system.
In all, some 200,000 Floridians were either not permitted to vote in the November 7 election on questionable or possibly illegal grounds, or saw their ballots discarded and not counted. A large and disproportionate number were black."

Whenever there is any close call to decide on an elected candidate, what is the normal practice? Recount the votes again to the satisfaction of all concerned. But, what happened in Florida?

As per, *http://www.gregpalast.com/detail.cfm?artid=29&row=1*:

"Palm Beach voting machines misread 27,000 ballots. Jeb Bush's Secretary of State, Katharine Harris, stopped them counting these votes by hand. She did the same to Gadstone, one of Florida's blackest, poorest and most Democrat counties, where machines failed to count one in eight ballots. Again Harris stopped the hand count. This alone cost Gore another 700 votes, in an election in which Harris declared George Bush winner by only 537 votes."

Let us try and summarize what happened based on the information available in numerous sources.

Governor Bush and Katherine Harris used illegal and immoral means to eliminate many voters who are likely to vote for democrats.

Inadequate and incompetent electoral system (voting machines and ballots) was in place in various counties.Let me quote the following from *http://www.gregpalast.com/detail.cfm?artid=29&row=1* and *Stupid White Men* respectively:

• "Whacky butterfly ballots caused thousands in this Democrat town to accidentally mess up, and they were refused replacement ballots promised them by state law."

• "Thus, the Palm Beach Post estimates that more than 3,000 voters, mostly elderly and Jewish, who thought they were voting for Al Gore ended up punching the wrong hole – for Pat Buchanan. Even Buchanan went on TV to declare that, "no way in hell did those Jewish voters vote for him."

What is up with America? Is it a developing country that is not used to new technology yet? For heaven's sake, we have already sent men to the moon. We manufacture precision weapons that use state of the art technology. Of late, Mr. Bush expressed his desire to use taxpayer's money on exploration of Mars. Is that your immediate priority when millions are still homeless and starving, and when the voting system in USA is stinking? As for the intellectuals and scientists, we have the best of the best living in this country. Can't we afford to define, design and install one of the best and unique foolproof electoral systems throughout the country that will register and report accurately and immediately the data on *who voted for whom*? Is it something America cannot afford to spend money on, or is it something that is not that important to worry about? According to me, in the interest of democracy, this is the #1 priority project that the Federal government must implement in every state well before the next election.

Okay, Mr. Bush, you may not be keen on getting competitive quotes from various sources in this context, even though it involves our tax money. Go ahead and give this contract to one of your buddies like Halliburton, if you like, as you did with other Government contracts. We don't mind. All we don't want is for the entire world to laugh at us **again** during the next election time. We want the rest of the world to regard and respect us again ,like how they used to do before. We are ashamed of what happened in year 2000 Presidential election, and more so ashamed of the way you got to the White House. In every sense of the word, it is a disgrace and immoral. Do you have something called conscience? Do you really believe in God? Honestly if you do, when you pray to God, don't you feel guilty about the way you made your move to the White House?

Besides, do you, the citizens, remember watching on TV the votes recounting episode in Florida and a set of thugs screaming and shouting outside the counting offices with a view to stop the recount? By the way, who are they? Are they sort of honest citizens of the Florida state trying to restore the democracy in Florida?

Please checkout the website, *http://www.alternet.org/ story.html?StoryID=10188*, for information on this. I copy herein a relevant section for your ready reference. "What if House Republican majority whip Tom Delay was not an evil genius? After a non-decisive Election Day, the Gore camp rolled out the lawyers, as did the Bush team; Delay mobilized two hundred or so Republican staffers and dispatched his khaki-clad foot soldiers to Miami. They swarmed the county office where a recount was under way, screamed and yelled, and created a disruptive and tense atmosphere in which the local election canvassing board then decided to cease the recount. In a wonderful piece of investigative journalism, Washington Post columnist Al Kamen -- who pens a gossipy who's-doing-what-in-official-Washington feature -- printed a photo of the GOP mob in Miami and asked his readers to identify the angry demonstrators. Of the twelve protesters pictured, ten were present or recent House Republican aides. The guy leading the pack: Tom Pyle, was a policy analyst for Delay."

I would strongly urge you to checkout all the sources cited above, if you really want to know what is wrong with our democracy.

If a Democratic Party election official carried out these atrocities, that individual would have already been put in jail for a very long time. But, what happened to Katherine Harris? Jail? Censure? Dismissal? No. She got elected to US Congress in year 2002 as a reward for all the noble services she did to your state. Don't you think your democracy is stinking in Florida? What is the matter with you, the citizens of Florida? Are you all really out of your mind? Have you no conscience? While you pray to God, don't you feel guilty for what you citizens have, or have not done to maintain a decent democracy in your state?

Because of the unnecessary and unjustified recent Iraq invasion and continued occupation, ever increasing numbers of our young men and women of this great nation have already died or been seriously wounded, and still continue to face that danger in Iraq now. Please checkout the website, *http:/*

/www.truthout.org/docs 03/111603H.shtml.

Besides the American casualties, **countless** number of innocent Iraqi civilians, including women and children, were, and are being killed or seriously wounded because of the American invasion and occupation. Maybe, this is not that important for us to worry about since we care about Americans only, but not Iraqis. Is that what it is? I hold you all responsible for that. You folks were just silent, sitting and watching everything that went on in November and December 2000. You did nothing positive in a peaceful but powerful way when the GOP inflicted the evil acts in Florida on your democracy. It is worth noting here a relevant statement by Edmund Burke: "All that is necessary for evil to triumph is for good men to do nothing." That is what happened, dear American citizen. You did nothing. So, we are suffering now and will continue to suffer, if we don't wake up at least now. The ball is right there in your court. Realize the past mistake. Don't repeat it again. Please use your head and stay focussed to eradicate the evils from power.

Let me cite an instance while I was growing up in India. At that time, a lot of Indians were blaming the British for everything that happened to India. My response to them was "What were *we* doing?" British always believed and practised the "divide and rule" policy effectively. Remember the saying, "united we stand, but, divided we fall." We were not smart, but also, we were sleeping. We were illiterate, ignorant, and indifferent to what was going on around us in spite of our sufferings. We waited for Mahatma Gandhi to wake us all up, and show us, and the world, the most powerful, but peaceful, way to get rid of the British from India." This was my answer to my fellow Indians then. So, please let us not just blame the politicians for the present sad state of affairs. They have, and will continue, to take us for a ride. It is up to us to wake up, and do the right things at the right time, in the right way. Crying baby gets the milk.

The Judiciary Branch is the Supreme Court. It is responsible to interpret the laws of the land, the supreme law of the land being the Constitution. The Supreme Court has the ultimate power to decide on how a law is interpreted and executed. The President nominates the Supreme Court judges and then, with the consent of the Senate, appoints them.

Here also, having witnessed what happened in Year 2000 Presidential election, we note a serious problem. The Florida state Supreme Court judges (**mostly with political affiliation to the democrats**) instructed the state government to continue the vote recounts. But, the ultimate authority, viz. US Supreme Court judges (**mostly with political affiliation to the Republicans**) instructed the state to stop the vote recounting, effective immediate, so that Mr. Bush can be declared the winner.

Let us have a brief look into what happened here. As you are aware, as of year 2000, there were nine US Supreme Court Judges, seven judges nominated by the Republican Presidents and two judges nominated by the Democratic President.

The following **five** judges voted **for** stopping the recount:

1. Anthony Kennedy   (Nominated by Republican President)
2. Sandra Day O'Connor   (Nominated by Republican President)
3. William Rehnquist   (Nominated by Republican President)
4. Antonin Scalia   (Nominated by Republican President)
5. Clarence Thomas   (Nominated by Republican President)

The following **four** judges voted **against** stopping the recount:

1. Stephen Breyer   (Nominated by Democratic President)
2. Ruth Bader Ginsburg   (Nominated by Democratic President)
3. David Souter   (Nominated by **Republican** President)
4. John Paul Stevens   (Nominated by **Republican** President)

Please note that two judges, viz. David Souter and John Paul Stevens, who were nominated by former Republican Presidents wanted the recounting to continue.

Let us see what they said in this respect. As per the website, *http://www.cnn.com/2000/ALLPOLITICS/stories/12/09/president.election/,*

"Justice Stevens accused the majority of acting 'unwisely,'" and wrote, "Preventing the recount from being completed will inevitably cast a cloud on the legitimacy of the election."

As for the Justice Souter's remarks, according to the website, *http://*

www.megalaw.com/election2000/ussc121200souter.php, "There is no justification for denying the State the opportunity to try to count all disputed ballots now."

So, it appears as if Justice Stevens and Justice Souter, even though nominated by Republican Presidents, really cared for the survival of the democracy. We sincerely thank them for the same. But, as for the other five justices, perhaps being loyal to their political affiliation and agenda was more important than ensuring proper functioning of the democracy. Hope they are able to sleep all right at night. God only knows.

In my opinion, those five US Supreme Court judges did not weigh the people's interests first. But, instead they chose to show their loyalty to the political party that put them there, but not to the people who pay them and whom they are supposed to serve and protect.

The present system of political nomination of judges is wrong in every sense of the word. Judges should be free from any sort of political persuasion and or affiliation. In general, there should be no nomination or appointment of any individual by any politician when it comes to the services (court of law, CIA, FBI, FEC, etc.) related to the people's interest. Besides, in view of the importance of the type of responsibility they have, to serve the people and not the politicians, it is important that they, too, retire at a well thought out retirement age, perhaps 70. Relevant Constitutional amendments are the only solutions to resolve these serious issues.

Government for the people.

The main purpose of the **Legislative Branch** is to make the laws, **with the consent of the people**, to ensure that the people's interests are protected and taken care of. I am afraid that we have a real serious problem here. As mentioned already in the "Introduction," the lobbyists seem to draft almost all the laws, and your elected members are kept in constant pressure by the lobbyists to enact them into laws. There is no pressure from you, the citizens who sent them there. So, what do you expect the outcome would be? Under this unpleasant situation, whose interests are due to be taken care of? You tell me. It is not that your elected members do not want to serve you. Of course, they do. But, the corrupt stinking system that is in place now prevents them from working for you.

Unless, and until, each and every one of you realize this serious problem, and do something really drastic and effective immediately to get rid of this corrupt practice for good, whether you believe it or not, you have no chance of realizing your real and true democracy. If you want your democracy to work for you, this is the first and foremost task you need to do.

Let us just recall this fact of life. Unless you are self-employed, most of you are working for an employer. In brief, what are you expected to do, in return for what you earn for living?

- Get to work on time and stay at work for the entire duration of your working hours.
- Concentrate on your assigned responsibilities at all times when you are at work to take care of the interests of your employer.
- Regularly report to your supervisor regarding your performance at work so that you can be assessed accordingly and appropriately.

These are the basic expectations from your employer. Your employer, through your supervisor, constantly monitors what you are doing or not doing. You know what happens, if you fail in any of these basic and justifiable expectations of your employer? You get fired. If you don't do your job properly, your employer has every right to throw you out.

Now, let us see what is happening in the case of the people's employees, viz. President/Prime Minister and legislatures.

When we watch the proceedings of the Parliament or Congress, most of the time the chamber is almost empty except on those occasions like the "Prime Minister's Question Time" and "President's Address to the Congress." We see just a few administrative staff of the chamber and the lonely legislator who wants to place on record that he/she said something in the chamber. Where are your other elected employees who are getting paid out of your tax money? Are they not supposed to listen to that member's speech in the chamber? Are they out partying with the vested interests? Are they not supposed to be in the chamber working for you while the session is on? Are they out on any vacation paid for by the vested interests? What is going on? If you are not at work during your normal working hours and if you are not working to take care of the interests of your employer, justifiably, you get fired. What happens to these legislators? Why aren't they working for you at all times as expected?

You know what happens, if you waste your working hours on gossips and doing unproductive things, instead of concentrating on your work at all times. Yes, you get fired, justifiably so. But, unfortunately, in the case of your elected employees of your government, they are just let loose, purely because you, the citizens, do not monitor and control what your candidate is up to. Are they reporting to you on a regular basis regarding their performance and activities?

For the life of me, I am yet to fathom out why anyone wants to be a member of the Congress or the President. I don't think that the salary is all that much. Then, what is it? What motivates and drives them towards this. Pardon me. What did you say? Oh! Please, don't give me a heart attack. They are not there to serve the people. We are yet to see the evidence to this aspect. Could it be that, they want to be in the public arena so that they are recognized, and possibly respected, in the respective community from where they get elected? Or, perhaps they manage to get a lot of other perks that we don't know about from the special interests? God only knows.

Just one more thing I want to mention here. Okay, you have been sweating and slogging away all the time, perhaps to hang on to your job, or hoping for some sort of pay increase based on your supervisor's recommendations. Poor you. Look what the situation is in the case of the members of your Legislative Branch who are nothing but your elected employees. Irrespective of whatever is the economic situation of the country, they can, and they do, make all the necessary arrangements to get their salary increased every year. This is in return for what? For doing an excellent job of protecting and taking care of your interests? Are you still in a deep coma? This is in return for being obedient to the lobbyists throughout their term of office, and repeating the mantras "yes, sir" and "yes, madam" to the lobbyists. My dear citizens, it is time to wake up and do everything that is needed to make them work for you and also to keep them well under your control. Don't forget the fact that they are there to serve you, and you are paying their wages. All along they have been let loose. It is time to keep them under your control, and not under the control of the lobbyists.

Let me cite another reason as to why I don't have any respect for any politician, whether they are a democrat or a republican. Do you recall Mr. John McCain giving all his reasons in the 2000 primaries as to why Mr. Bush is not the right person to be the President? The same Mr. McCain was campaigning for Mr. Bush in the New Hampshire area in January 2004. Can you believe it? These politicians know very well that most of us don't use our head and common sense in choosing our candidates. So, they exploit this fact of life and fool us all the time. My God. These politicians make me sick. Is there any single politician who really cares for the welfare of the people? Please let me know, if you come across anyone.

The websites *http://www.senate.gov* and *http://www.house.gov* give some information on what the members of the Congress are doing. These are government sites. So, honestly, I don't expect to get the facts on all we need to know about the performance of each member of the Congress. We need independent investigative reporters who watch these legislatures like hawks, and report regularly back to us on their findings.

If you, the citizens, do all you can to force each and every one of your elected employees to report to you on their performance and activities and you take appropriate action, if need be, to control their behaviour, then there is a real good chance for your democracy to succeed. Sadly, purely because you, the citizens, do not monitor and control their activities and performance, they are making laws that meet the requirements of the special interests who gave campaign contributions. This is a very serious problem.

Let me cite the following two relevant quotes:

1. "Corporations have taken over the government and turned it against its own people." - Ralph Nader

2. "I hope we shall crush in its birth the aristocracy of our moneyed corporations which dare already to challenge our government to a trial of strength and bid defiance to the laws of our country." - Thomas Jefferson, 3rd US president 1801-1809
Please checkout *http://www.corporations.org/campaign$$/*. This site

provides numerous links related to various aspects and activities of the corporations. In my opinion, this is very important and hence we must be aware of what is presented in these links. I identify herein just a few of those numerous links for your ready reference.

The site, *http://www.corporatecrimereporter.com/corruptreport.pdf,* gives a 16 pages report on *"Public Corruption in the United States."* This is a report released by *Corporate Crime Reporter* (National Press Club, Washington, D.C.) as of January 16, 2004. It is just another big eye opener to all of us.

As per the website, *http://www.thirdworldtraveler.com/ Controlling_Corporations/ControllingCorporations.html*, "I see in the near future a crisis approaching that unnerves me, and causes me to tremble for the safety of my country...corporations have been enthroned, and an era of corruption in high places will follow, and the money of the country will endeavor to prolong its reign by working upon the prejudices of the people until all wealth is aggregated in a few hands and the Republic is destroyed. I feel at this moment more anxiety for the safety of my country than ever before, even in the midst of war." - President Abraham Lincoln

What President Lincoln feared then, has been true all along, and you have the evidence even now, as of June 2004, when I finalize my manuscripts for this book.

Let me quote the following which is as per the website, http:// www.cbsnews.com/stories/2004/05/25/eveningnews/printable619558.shtml, "It's no secret that when it comes to the mounting cost of security for all high-risk terrorist targets, like nuclear power plants and railroads, there simply isn't enough Homeland Security money to go around.

But, as CBS News Correspondent Mika Brzezinski reports, precious taxpayer dollars are quietly going to pay for security at some of the richest corporations in the world. Major oil companies have received $65 million to buy cameras, fencing, and communications equipment. "We don't have unlimited resources," says Danielle Brian, the executive director of Project On Government Oversight. Brian cites the Bush administration's close ties with the oil industry and points out that these companies could well afford to pay for their own security.

"They're taking absolute advantage of the situation, and the government is letting them get away with it," said Brian.

"Case in point: Citgo made a $439 million profit but took $19.4 million in government grants. ConocoPhillips earned $4.7 billion in profits but received nearly $10.8 million. ChevronTexaco netted a whopping $7.2 billion profit, but several of its facilities still got over $7.3 million in government handouts."

Our firefighters and police personnel who protect and serve us did not get sufficient funds from the Homeland Security department, but Mr. Bush's rich buddies in the oil industry managed to get our tax dollars in spite of the sizable profit they made. Wake up, America.

As per, http://www.corporations.org/system/ the following can be noted:

• Of the world's 100 largest economic entities, 51 are now corporations and 49 are countries. (See chart)
• The world's top 200 corporations account for over a quarter of economic activity on the globe while employing less than one percent of its workforce. (Source)
• The richest 1 percent of Americans own 40 percent of the nation's household wealth (as of 1997). (Source)
• The assets of the world's 358 billionaires exceed the combined annual incomes of countries with 45 percent of the world's people. (Source)
• The average CEO in the U.S. made 42 times the average workers pay in 1980, 85 times in 1990 and 531 times in 2000. (Source)
• The courts have given corporations the basic Constitutional rights of persons, but workers lose those rights on entering the workplace.
• The corporate share of taxes paid has fallen from 33 percent in the 1940's to 15 percent in the 1990's. Individuals' share of taxes has risen from 44 to 73 percent.
• The World Trade Organization effectively gives corporations veto power over our U.S. environmental and labor laws, weakening our right to protect ourselves and our land through our legislation.
I fully agree with Mr. Ross Perot when he said, "The system is corrupt,

not the people in it."

As per the website, *http://www.issues2000.org/Celeb/ Ross_Perot_Government_Reform.htm*, "Perot believes that the chief problem in America is not corrupt people in a good system, but good people in a corrupt system. Our system of government is the problem. We've got to change the system. I'm critical of the system and not individuals. I have said that you could replace everybody in Congress, find the best people in the country, put them in that system, and in months they'd look just like the people you're replacing." - *Source: Strong-Man Politics, by George Grant, p.108-9 Nov 7, 1992.*

The Center for Responsive Politics is a non-partisan, non-profit research group based in Washington, D.C. that tracks money in politics, and its effect on elections and public policy. The Center conducts computer-based research on campaign finance issues for the news media, academics, activists, and the public at large. The Center's work is aimed at creating a more educated voter, an involved citizenry, and a more responsive government.

This center's website is http://www.opensecrets.org. This is one of the best sources to learn about the influence of money in U.S. politics. This provides numerous links to various topics that we as citizens must know to find out the corrupt influence of money on Federal governments, politics and election. For proper functioning of democracy we need to educate ourselves by learning where the problems are. This site will be of immense help in this context.

For similar information on the state and local levels we can use the website, *http://www.followthemoney.org.*

Use the "Who Gives" and "Who Gets" sections of the website, *http:// www.opensecrets.org,* to find information on lobbyists, members of Congress, political action committees, among other things. In their *"News"* section, they have various articles summarizing their data as well as providing a more detailed background of the industries and contribution trends.

A few sections of this site, that I think we must be kept informed, are cited below:

The website, *http://www.opensecrets.org/bigpicture/ statetotals.asp?cycle=2002* provides "The Big Picture" of "*The Money Behind the Elections*" in terms of the "*Contributions by State*" for the Election Cycle 2002. Please checkout the percentage of the contributions in each state in favour of the party of its choice. A total of 42 states to the Republicans whereas just 9 states to the Democrats. The information is based on the data released by the Federal Election Commission (FEC) on Monday, June 09, 2003. The totals include Political Action Committee (PAC), soft money and individual contributions to federal candidates and parties.

The site *http://www.opensecrets.org/pacs/topacs.asp* provides the data on the top 20 PAC contributors to Federal Candidates in 2003-2004 who paid to both the parties, and it shows the respective percentages in terms of their preference. For example, Wal-Mart paid 16% to the Democrats and 84% to the Republicans. A study of this list provides interesting information in respect of who prefers whom. Obviously, Wal-Mart management relies on Republicans better to get their interests attended to. Also, please note, Machinists / Aerospace Workers Union paid 98% to the Democrats whereas just 1% to the Republicans. What does this mean? These workers obviously hope to get their interests taken care of better by the Democrats than by the Republicans. Besides, look at the data on those who paid significant percentage to each party. For example, American Bankers Association paid 39% to the Democrats and 61% to the Republicans. What does it signify? They trust the Republicans better to take care of their interests. But, at the same time, they do not wish to rub the Democrats on the wrong side. This way, if it comes to the crunch, their lobbyist can twist the arms of the democrats also to vote in their favour. Unlike us, the ordinary citizens, these vested interests are really sharp, smart and shrewd. They have built in a sort of safety cushion to get the things done TO THEIR ADVANTAGE, let whatever be the political climate, using the people whom YOU elected to take care of YOUR INTERESTS.

The site *http://www.opensecrets.org/pacs/topacs.asp?txt=D&cycle=2004* provides the list of top 20 PAC contributors from whom the Democrats received more money. Obviously, they are mainly the members of the trade unions and other workers unions.

The site *http://www.opensecrets.org/pacs/topacs.asp?txt=R&cycle=2004*

provides the list of top 20 PAC contributors from whom the Republicans received more money. Obviously, they are mainly from the big corporations or employers.

Until I started collecting information for this book, I had no clue as to what PAC or soft money means. All I have been concerned with is the fact that our elected representatives are bought and bullied by the vested interests on both sides of the political spectrum. As such, the functioning of both Legislative and Executive branches of government both stink to the core.

The site *http://www.opensecrets.org/pacs/topacs.asp?txt=R&cycle=2004* provides an insight into what PAC means.

The site *http://www.opensecrets.org/pubs/glossary/softmoney.htm* provides interesting information on soft money.

The site *http://www.opensecrets.org/overview/topcontribs.asp?Bkdn=DemRep&Cycle=2004* provides the list of top 100 donors to both the parties.

Please do checkout this table and in particular the comments *"Contributions Tilt"* made by the Centre for Responsive Politics in the last column of the table. Look at the names of all those (Goldman Sachs, National Association of Realtors, Lehman Brothers, Microsoft Corporations, National Rural Electric Cooperative Association, Northrop Grumman, Akin, Gump et al, Cassidy & Associates/Interpublic Group, Bank One Corporation, Altria Group, Chicago Merchantile Exchange, Metropolitan Life, and General Motors) who are "on the fence." It is very interesting indeed. Aren't they clever? They don't have to worry about which party controls the power. Their vested interests are duly taken care of irrespective of whosoever may be in charge of making the laws.

The site *http://www.opensecrets.org/overview/topcontribs.asp?Bkdn=Source&Cycle=2004* provides the list of same 100 top donors. But, the details are presented in terms of what percentage to PAC, Soft Money and Individuals.

There are so many links available in *www.opensecrets.org* to educate us in this area where corruption and bribery dominates beyond anybody's imagination. Obviously, I cannot bring forth each and every detail in this context. All I want to emphasize and bring to your attention here, is just this: the system is corrupt to the core. Your elected candidates are under constant pressure by the lobbyists to ensure that their interests are enacted as laws. We, the citizens, just watch and do NOTHING.

Having briefed a bit about the behaviour of the Legislative Branch of your government, now let us spend some time to find out what the situation is with the Executive Branch of your government. Is your Executive Branch really working for you and taking care of your interests? The answer is another emphatic "NO."

Please don't forget the following facts.

Who is the Vice President? Dick Cheney, the former CEO of Halliburton. Who got most of the major rebuilding contracts where our tax money is spent? Halliburton. No competitive quotes were called for from other sources. Can you believe it? It can happen only in Bush's American Democracy.

Who is the White House Chief of Staff? It is none other than the former chief lobbyist of the General Motors. So, where will the other government contracts go? Obviously they will go to please other lobbyists.

So, what do you see here with the CEO of your government? The former CEO of Halliburton is next in command, and the former chief lobbyist is in charge of everything that happens in the White House. Besides, it has been reported that no other candidate in the American history has ever collected so much of campaign contributions from all sorts of special interests like what Mr. Bush has done, till now. Just a minute, it is not over yet. He might not have had all the expected "thank you" contributions from all those millionaires and billionaires who received massive tax cuts from him. I'm sure that Mr. Bush's name will go very well in the Guinness Book of Records in this respect. Why do these special interests pour so much money on Mr. Bush's winning? Don't you get it? Most of those selfish people who have no conscience, or concern for the welfare of the innocent, poor citizens who vote for him. But, in turn, Bush will pay back the special interests through all sorts of government contracts. Aren't we the real suckers? Need I say any more on his "working for the people?" Yes, I have some more to say in this context in other chapters as well.

Let me qualify what I mean by taking care of "your interests."

When I say "your interest," I mean the interests of those homeless and starving citizens, but not the interests of the richest 1 percent who own 40 % of the nations household wealth.

When I say "your interest," I mean the interests of the poor, weak and vulnerable, but not the interests of those top executives of the corporations who make fortunes by way of salary, stock options, bonuses, and what not.

When I say "your interest," I mean the interests of those naive and innocent people who are unable to help themselves, but not the interests of those 358 billionaires whose assets exceed the combined annual incomes of the countries with 45% of the world's people.

When I say "your interest," I mean the interests of most of us, the ordinary hard working citizen who pay tax through our nose, but not the interests of those big corporations who have smart and shrewd tax specialists who can find ways to pay little or no tax at all.

I am really surprised, shocked, sad and sick, when I hear that still some people really believe that Mr. Bush is doing a good job as the President.

This is in spite of him, as per Richard Clarke, failing to protect the Americans from 9/11 attacks, even though all the evidences were presented to him well in advance.

This is in spite of him failing to give the facts on the 9/11 episodes to the commission **under oath, on official record**. He was reluctant, but forced to initiate this commission by the families of the 9/11 victims. If he has really nothing to hide, why can't he give the interview under oath like others in his Cabinet did?

This is in spite of him, instead of concentrating on the 9/11 terrorists, invading Iraq while there was no proven imminent threat from Saddam Hussein.

This is in spite of him being the cause for the ever-increasing numbers of the deaths of our young men and women and the large number of the innocent Iraqi civilians including women and children.

This is in spite of the fact that he has reversed the surplus status of our country's economy to a disastrous deficit status, where our children and our grandchildren will have to work hard to pay back the country's debt.

By the way, if you want to keep an eye on what the outstanding public debt as of every day, check out in *http://www.brillig.com/debt_clock/*. Besides that, this site provides other links with information about what sort of burden we are passing on to our children and grandchildren. Normally, we try our best to save whatever we can and pass them on to our kids for their future. Mr. Bush and Mr. Cheney need not have to worry about this happening to their kids when they increase our national debt by giving real good tax cut to the millionaires and billionaires, by taking the country to war in Iraq when there was no justification at all for this invasion, and also by returning the favours to the drug manufacturers and insurance companies through the recent Medicare Prescription Bill. As for Mr. Bush and Mr. Cheney, the national debt does not matter that much. But, it does to us, and to our children, and grandchildren.

As per, *http://www.cbsnews.com/stories/2004/03/15/eveningnews/printable606477.shtml,*

"An e-mail -- obtained by CBS News -- appears to show the White House was anxious to hide ballooning cost estimates. Sent on behalf of former Medicare administrator Tom Scully, it warns the agency's chief actuary, Rick Foster to not tell Congress the price tag would be well above the White House's stated 400 billion.

Foster is told, "the consequences for insubordination are extremely severe...."

Mr. Bush, you keep saying that your tax cut is the real reason for the improvement in economy, if there is any improvement. Tell this to the millions who are still desperately searching for jobs. Why don't you publish the figures on how many of those millionaires and billionaires who benefited extremely well from your tax cuts really invested this money back into the business in the interest of the economy? I'm sure, they would have put that money away somewhere safe for the rainy days, may be even in Swiss banks. Nobody knows what is in store. Anything can happen like what happened to your close buddy, Ken Lay of Enron.

What happened to our freedom of speech, Mr. Bush? In preparation for your travel around the country, your Secret Service visits the location ahead of time and orders local police to set up "free speech zones" or "protest zones" where people opposed to your policies are quarantined. These zones keep the protesters out of presidential sight and outside the view of media covering the event. Why are you so scared to find out what people think of your policies? Do you want to see and mingle with only those people who support your policies? Is this the democracy you want to preach, practice and impose in Iraq also now?

Numerous instances can be cited where injustice was done to these citizens who want you to know how they feel about your policies. Why don't you have the courage to face the people at large and answer to their concerns and anxieties, like how your partner in crime, Mr. Tony Blair regularly does in Parliament and television shows? He takes all sorts of questions from the citizens and answers them. Why can't you do the same, if you are truly convinced of what you are doing is right for the country, and the people at large in respect of their living conditions?

Mr. Blair is the real man with courage and conviction even though he is bullied into supporting you. How much I wish I could the say the same about you, too. But, unfortunately, I am still sane and can identify right from wrong. The recent episode of your interview with the 9/11 commission members, along with Mr. Cheney, is just another example in this context. By the way, did you hold Cheney's hand for comfort and relaxation while you were talking to the members of the 9/11 commission? For heaven's sake, you are supposed to be the Commander in Chief of the mightiest military force this planet earth has ever had; you are the selected, but not elected, leader of one of the greatest nations on this planet. No wonder the rest of the world is laughing at your intellectual ability as you face the people and press, on your own, without any notes or speech prepared by your staff.

I can go on and on, citing so many facts on all Mr. Bush did to the rich and did not do to the ordinary people. All I can think of in this context at this moment is just this. The people who seem to support Mr. Bush should fall into the following categories, viz.

• The right wing extremists who believe and practice in America dominating the rest of the world, giving good tax cut to the rich and spending the taxpayer's money to dig dirt and derail democrats like how they did to the Clintons all the time, ever since the Clintons moved to the White House.
• The people who are reasonably well off and believe and practice the concept of "survival of the fittest." According to these people, "I come first" and "we need cheap oil." "Me, me and me." "If Bush is prepared to give me some tax cut, then he gets my vote." That is all they care about. As such, they want to do whatever it takes to get what they want, whether it is justifiable and moral or not.
• The people who, for some reason or other, can't stand democrats.
• The people who get carried away by the small tax cut that Mr. Bush offers at the expense of the citizen's welfare.
• The people who are still in deep illusion, and blindly believe in the preaching and false promises of Mr. Bush's administration.
• The people who are either unable or unwilling to use their head and common sense to reason out the real serious and sombre status of the nation.

I admit, I am not aware of anything good that Mr. Bush did to uplift the living conditions of homeless, starving, poor, weak, vulnerable, naive, innocent, and ordinary, hard-working, low and middle income group of citizens. As such, I ask each and every one of those who still think that Mr. Bush is doing a good job to take a deep breath, close their eyes, pray to God, and convince their own conscience, not anybody else, by giving one simple fact to prove that Mr. Bush did something positive to uplift the living conditions of the type of people that I mentioned above. Let me repeat again, you don't have to convince me or anybody else. Assuming you really believe in God, and you do have a conscience, you convince your own conscience to help you sleep better at night.

I'm so sorry, Mr. Bush, I take back everything that I said about you. You are a compassionate conservative. I forgot about that. Anyway, you don't owe anything to these ordinary citizens. Because, the fact is most of these people did not elect you to be the President. You got into the White House with the help of your brother in Florida and your father's powerful friends in the US Supreme Court. As such, what you are doing is just right. You owe nothing to these people. They don't deserve anything from you, because most of them preferred Mr. Gore. You continue to help your rich buddies by giving tax cuts to all those who made, and make, quite a lot of campaign contribution to you and GOP. As everyone knows, money talks. So, you accumulate as much as you possibly can since you need it to spend on publicity and false propaganda to fool the people again. Most of us are still blind and believe everything you say. You continue injecting that fear of terrorists all the time, and tell the people that you are the only one who can contain the terrorists, even though you don't do a damn thing to understand, and minimise, if not eliminate, the root cause for these terrorist activities, viz. the answers to the following questions:
   • **Why do they do what they do?** In the interest of the safety and security of this great nation, did you bother to explore and find out what their grievances and complaints are, and try to do something about it? As per Richard Clarke, you ignored all the warnings.
   • Why do they attack mostly the American and Israeli interests and the interests of those countries who were bullied into support you?
   • Did you bother to find out why these young terrorists, both men and women, resort to kill themselves while they kill other innocent victims? Of course, they are brainwashed. No doubt. But, do they have anything better to hope and live for? Don't you see that they are desperate?
   • **Even after having had bitter lessons from Vietnam War, don't you still realize that mighty military can only win the war but not the hearts and minds of the people?**

Most of the people here don't use their head, any way. So, you can buy them off and get their popular votes also next time. You are on the right track to extend your present occupation in 1600 Pennsylvania Avenue. Keep it up. You are just one of a kind. The future is bright for you, since most of us continue NOT to be that sharp, smart and shrewd in figuring out what you are up to. This is because we are still dumb.

By the way, John Kerry is not an angel either. As per Tim Russert's interview with John Kerry, *http://www.msnbc.msn.com/id/4772030/*, his policy towards the Middle East and Iraq war is not all that different to that of Mr. Bush. He, too, blindly supports Israeli's arrogant approach to resolve the Palestinian issues and he doesn't admit that the war in Iraq is a mistake.

My ideal choice is for independent people like Ross Perot and Ralph Nader. But, we have to be realistic and be aware of the present political system. In the absence of a powerful third party, like how it is in the United Kingdom, I am aware that **any vote to Ralph Nader will be a vote down the drain**. As such, now we have two evils with a chance to become the President of this great nation. So, we have to weigh everything they say regarding all the issues facing the world, and us. We need to make our choice on the lesser of the two evils and, according to me, it is John Kerry, whether I like it or not. The ordinary working class people may **hope** to have a better living condition with Kerry in the White House since Mr. Bush is a proven disaster.

I have been repeating quite a lot, like a parrot, about taking care of the people's interests. What are those interests? We all have our own needs and wants. First of all, our basic needs must be provided for. As for our wants, sky is the limit and there is no end to it. According to me, the people's interests must, first of all, relate to the basic needs of the poor, weak, and vulnerable, and those who are unable to help themselves, and then the needs of ordinary citizens like you and me who belong to the low or middle income group. Most of your buddies and favourites viz. the top 1% of the rich population and executives of big corporations, know how to take care of themselves. They are extremely good at it. Of course, you are there to do whatever it takes to help them. I am talking about the rest of the majority of the population that is wondering and worrying all the time where to find the money to pay the bills and feed the family. Let us look at some of these needs.

Don't you think it is a disgrace that a civilized government is not really doing anything positive and effective to provide decent shelters to the millions of homeless people, and provide basic food to the millions of starving people? Do they have to rely on charitable organisations for their food and shelter? They are also our fellow citizens. What happened to one of the basic but the most important statement in the Declaration of Independence, viz. "all men are created equal"? Is it not valid anymore? Or is it that America, or for that matter any civilized country, cannot afford to allocate resources to solve this shameful situation? No, that is not the case. As far as the dirty politicians are concerned, it is not that important, and it is not in their priority list. These politicians are not starving and they are not homeless. As such, it does not affect them directly. Does it? Who cares?

Of course, out of these homeless and starving people, there may be quite a number of lazy lots who may not want to do any work for their food and shelter. Your government must do everything appropriate in respect of eliminating this situation. If you see even a single homeless and starving soul on the street, it is a shame on you and me. This group of people must be taken off the street, provided with at least some sort of basic food and shelter, and forced to do whatever work they can in return for the food and shelter being provided. Like all of us, they too must be made to earn for their living. Something positive must be done to make them get their dignity and self-respect back.

Having identified my top most priority item first, now let us see what possibly would be the basic needs of most of us who are not all that well off financially. According to me, the following could be the fundamental basic needs:

• We need a decent job where we can use whatever skills we may have, education, experience and expertise, to earn enough income to have a roof over us, food to eat, educate our children and pay the bills.

• We need a decent habitable home, preferably own it, in a safe and secured environment where we don't have to worry about robbery, mugging, thieving and murder.

• We need a well-established educational system, schools, and support to prepare the future citizens of our country as loving, caring, and sharing type. Excellent educational opportunities must not be confined just to the rich only, but must be available for all to access.

• We need universal healthcare system for **ALL.** We should not have to debate and decide whether to pay for the normal household bills or the exorbitant health care bills.
I'm sure, there may be still so many other basic needs that I am not aware

of to list herein. I leave it to the experts in the respective fields to identify all the remaining.

Okay, we noted what the democracy means in theory and why the democracy is not functioning the way it is meant to function. Who is responsible for this miserable failure? Let us explore this aspect in detail now.

At the outset, whether you like it or not, I blame YOU, the citizens, for this failure. YES, it is YOU, the reader, who should take full responsibility for this failure. Do you know why? You are blessed with the most powerful tool: a vote. With this you control your own destiny, and that of others, by electing the candidates of your choice to serve you in your government. So, if you have not exercised this privileged right **carefully**, properly and effectively, and then make adequate arrangements to monitor and control their behaviour constantly, then there is no point in you constantly whining, groaning and moaning blaming others all the time for the present sad and sick state of the affairs.

The entire world was justifiably laughing at the American democracy when they witnessed the way the American President was decided in the year 2000; by five Supreme Court Judges who were appointed by the former Republican Presidents. What happened to the fundamental and basic principle of the democracy, viz. **government by the people**?

Besides, what did you, the American people, do when Mr. Bush recently invaded, and is still occupying, Iraq under false pretext? The entire world is still angry with Americans since you collectively did not stop this invasion. For heaven's sake, please realize this. You have the real power, and it is your government. The President and the members of Congress are your employees. You are not doing anything to monitor and control their behaviour. They are let loose. They do what they please. There is nothing you are doing about it.

This is the root cause for the failure of your democracy. **You do not have any effective system to constantly monitor and control the performance and activities of your candidates who are nothing but your employees and servants.** You are silent even while you suffer. What do you expect then? The evils take you for a ride and continue to screw you. I will repeat again the relevant statement by Edmund Burke, viz. "All that is necessary for evil to triumph is for good men to do nothing." You must raise your voice to be heard loud and clear.

I'm sure, there may be numerous reasons for this pathetic failure of your democracy. Only the historians and the political experts can fathom them out by digging out the details. As briefed before, I'm not an expert on politics. But, at the same time, I am educated and experienced enough to identify rights from wrongs. As such, as an ordinary citizen, I can think of the following three reasons for the failure:

1. You did not vote to elect a candidate of your choice to serve your government.

2. May be **you did vote**. But, did you elect your candidate after giving the due serious consideration to the candidate's credentials in respect of protecting your interests or you just blindly believed the candidate's promises and voted for that person?

3. Whether you voted or not, once the candidate is sent to serve you, do you really **monitor the performance and activities of your candidates** constantly and take appropriate action in the event of failure to carry out his/ her duty?

Let us explore each of these three items a bit more in detail now.

Prior to going into details on this subject, it is worth considering the following quotes by our former leaders and legends like Abraham Lincoln, Thomas Paine, John Kennedy, Dwight Eisenhower and Woodrow Wilson:

- "Freedom is the last best hope of earth" - Abraham Lincoln
- "… Our fathers brought forth on this continent a new nation, conceived in liberty and dedicated to the proposition that all men are created equal" - Abraham Lincoln
- "Those who expect to reap the blessings of freedom must, like men, undergo the fatigue of supporting it" – Thomas Paine
- "Ask not what your country can do for you; ask what you can do for your country" – John Kennedy

- "Only our individual faith in freedom can keep us free"
– Dwight Eisenhower
- "America is not anything if it consists of each of us. It is something only if it consists of all of us" – Woodrow Wilson

You did not vote.

If you did not vote, then the first question is, are you eligible to vote?

If you are **not eligible to vote YET**, the very fact that you are reading this book shows that you do care about yourself, your family, your community and your country. Even though you are unable to vote yet, please realize that your own present and future life heavily rests on the eligible voters in your neighbourhood casting their votes on the right candidates. So, the fact that you are not eligible to vote yet does not get you off the hook.

So, what can you do, as a good caring citizen, to protect everybody's interests in your neighbourhood? Essentially there are two most valuable services you can do.

1. **Do everything you can to get each and every eligible voter in your community to register, and vote.** One of the primary reasons for the failure of democracy is the poor voter turnout. A lot of people have the attitude of "I can't be bothered, I am busy otherwise, and I have no time to go and vote." Please remember, **every vote must count,** especially after what we witnessed in Florida in 2000 Presidential election. It is extremely important to make every eligible voter realize this fact. If only you can dedicate and devote yourself to minimise, if not eliminate, this serious problem of poor voter turnout, then you have laid a sound and solid ground for proper functioning of your democracy. Even though you couldn't vote yet, you do your part as a good and noble citizen by helping the eligible voters to vote. Excellent voter turnout is extremely important. Make it a point to find out whether all the eligible voters in your neighbourhood have registered to vote. On the Election Day, if any of the registered voters in your neighbourhood is unable to go to the voting booth because of any health problem or lack of transport, etc., please do all you can to get that neighbour to the voting booth. Use your God given intelligence, imagination, initiative and enthusiasm to devise all the possible ways and means to get every eligible voter in your area to vote.

You and your friends can go door to door to find out from your neighbours, well in advance, whether they are planning to go and vote or not, and whether they need any help, either in educating them to choose the right candidate, or taking them to the voting booth, etc. Perhaps, you can draft a brief note, something similar to what I drafted at the end of this chapter, and circulate it in your neighbour hood. Use your imagination and initiative to do everything you can to get them to vote. In spite of all these efforts, it is possible that the response from your neighbours may not be all that encouraging to the level of your expectations, and you may feel despondent that you slaved for nothing. Please, please don't feel depressed like that. You have proven to yourself and to the world that you have done a good job as a caring citizen. Please continue to participate in your grass root effort to eliminate the existing problem of the poor voter turnout. Never give up in what you are doing. You continue to make a difference by carrying out the noble task that you have undertaken to do. It means a lot to your society, and to your country.

2. The second thing is, everyone in your neighbourhood may not be as bright and intellectual as you are in understanding what is wrong with the present situation. As such, in the interest of everyone around you, please volunteer to educate the people in your neighbourhood, explaining what you think is the right approach to resolve all those problems at hand. Please do all you can to educate and persuade the eligible voters to exercise their right to elect a person of his/her choice. Also, your neighbours may still be undecided in respect of whom to elect. So, please help your neighbour to make the right choice, but definitely don't impose your idea of who is the right candidate. Explain the pros and cons in respect of each candidate. Let your neighbour decide based on whatever his/her expectations are. This is meant to be a real democracy. I have given, at the end of this chapter, a brief on what I expect from my candidates (see, **What I want my candidate to promise to do for me?**) Please refer to that section for guidelines, if need be, in respect of making the right choice.

In this context, I hope and pray that you are not an extremist with your political persuasion or religion. If you are, I don't like you, even though I respect you for your own views and thoughts. Please, be a moderate, but not an extremist, in the interest of the well being of everyone around you.

You are **eligible to vote, but did not vote**. Why not?

Did you register to vote? If you have not done it yet, you can find a lot of help from so many volunteers and the canvassing members of the contesting candidates in your area to get yourself registered to vote. Please remember, you have the powerful vote to control your own destiny and that of others in your neighbourhood. Your voting means and matters a lot to everyone around you. Please get yourself registered and make sure you vote.

Okay, you are eligible and registered to vote, but did not vote? Why not?

Are you one of those who have the attitude of, "I can't be bothered, I am busy otherwise and I have no time to go and vote?" As repeated many times before, please remember, **every vote must count.** We never know. Your vote could very well be the deciding vote. If you don't do your part to elect a candidate of your choice, then there is no point in you whining, moaning, and groaning all the time, and putting the blame on others for everything that is happening around you. You are to be blamed, not others. You must do your part, first. At least, this time, vote. You will find a lot of help from volunteers and the canvassing members of the contesting candidates in your area to help you with everything for you to vote. All you have to do is call one of them. They will even take you to the voting booth. There is so much of help available at your disposal. Please, please vote.

Could it be that you didn't vote because you don't know for whom to vote?

The candidate who is the best choice for me may not be the best choice for you. It depends on what your expectations are in respect of what you want your candidate to do for you. Just as an example, I have drafted, at the end of this chapter, a set of what my expectations are (see, **What I want my candidate to promise to do for me?**) You may please refer to that section for guidelines, if need be, and then write down what your expectations are. One thing we need to be clear on here: there is no point in expecting the candidate who contests the local county election to work towards making an amendment to the Constitution of the USA. We need to identify our requirements and expectations clearly in terms of local, state and federal levels. Having done that, then we must refer the right requirements list to the right candidate.

You did vote.

So, you did vote for a candidate of your choice. Did you make your choice carefully in line with whatever your expectations might have been from your candidate? Or you just blindly believed the candidate's promises and voted for that person? Anyway, there is no point in crying over the spilt milk. If you haven't done so last time, perhaps next time, you could consider making your choice wisely by following some of the guidelines cited above. Recently I watched the television news and interviews with the voters regarding the democratic primaries in various parts of the country. It was sad to note that no voter seems to have given any serious consideration on how to decide on a right candidate to vote for. If we the architects and pillars of the democracy take this matter so lightly, then there is no point in blaming the politicians for screwing us. We the people deserve what we have now. Success and prosperity will come to only those who get their priorities right and follow those priorities persistently. According to me, careful selection of the right candidate, whatever be your political persuasion, is the top most priority item for proper functioning of our democracy.

Monitoring the performance and activities of your candidate.

Whether you voted or not, we need to monitor the performance and activities of your candidates constantly, and take appropriate action in the event of failure to carry out his/her duty. This applies to all types of candidates, viz. President and members of the Congress in Federal level, and likewise in both state and local levels as well. At the moment, they are let loose. They are all puppets of the lobbyists who keep your elected candidates under constant pressure.

The recent behaviour of the republicans in all levels of governments (local, state and federal) in respect of the "gay marriage" issue makes me sick. I can't believe it. There are so many pressing and pending issues that need to be attended to without wasting any more of the precious legislative hours on "gay marriage." I can never forgive the republicans for the amount of time and taxpayers' money they wasted over the years while they were attempting to derail the Clintons and impeach former President Clinton, when they couldn't get all their judicial nominees accepted by the Senate, and above all the recent "gay marriage" issue. There are hundreds of top priority items that need to be attended to immediately. I sincerely hope and pray that every one of these irresponsible republicans are taught a lesson by the voters next time, like how the British voters taught lessons to the conservatives in England. We don't want irresponsible individuals who can't get their priorities right elected on our behalf. Let us pray to our Almighty to save this great nation from the clutches of the irresponsible republicans.

Let us summarize what I have been whining about till now in this chapter.

What did we learn from the year 2000 election episode in Florida? We don't want to face fraud activities again from the people like Katherine Harris, Jebb Bush and politically biased Supreme Court judges. So, it is obvious and imperative that we try and ensure to have the following concepts implemented:

• There should be no conflict of interest. So, every state should assign all the responsibilities associated with the election process to a civil servant who is independent and free from any political persuasion or affiliation. Besides, it would be ideal if that civil servant comes from another state.

• A reliable, proven and foolproof electronic voting system to register and report accurately and immediately the data on "who voted for whom" must be implemented in every state effective immediately.

• Media prediction of the election results must be delayed until all the votes are cast in all the states including Hawaii. There should be no earlier prediction to unduly influence the voters in the west.

• The Chief Executive Officer, viz. the President of your democratic government must represent the will of ALL the people. So, the President must be elected by the popular votes and NOT by the electoral votes.

• **Judiciary system should function free from any political influence. So, the present practice of political nomination of judges should be stopped. There should be an appropriate retirement age also for these judges. The concept of job forever, irrespective of their mental state of health as they get older, does not make any sense. The members of the Judiciary System must decide on the appointment of judges.**

As repeated before, the corporations have taken over the government and turned it against its own people. Again, the chief problem in America is not corrupt people in a good system, but good people in a corrupt system. Our system of government is the problem. We've got to change the system.
So, what do we do and how do we go about correcting the corrupt system? As for me, there are two steps. The 1st step is easy since it is entirely in your control. The 2nd step is not that easy, as our enemy here is the special interests who have all the resources, determination, and backing to continue the current status quo.

Step 1:

Clearly and calmly think through to identify and list all the issues that face you, your family, your community, your country and your world. You don't have to be a scholar to get this list produced. You know what you want in the interest of everyone around you. If need be, talk to the people whom you trust and get help to produce this list. It is possible that you may not be all that clear in defining what you want. Talk it over with your family, neighbors and the people with whom you closely associate with in your community and the places of worship, etc. Here you have to be vigilant and watch the activities of the extremists. They are very visible and forceful to impose their extremist ideas into you. Beware. You use your head. Listen to all the views and weigh all the inputs. Don't trust anyone. Having carefully considered all the inputs, produce separate lists of your requirements as appropriate for the local, state and federal level candidates. If need be, please checkout "**What I want my candidate to promise to do for me?**" given at the end of this chapter where I have listed, as an example, what I want my federal level candidate to do for me, my family, my community and my country.

Having got the respective lists for each contesting candidate, make each of these lists in the form of fliers for a wide circulation. You do the best you can to circulate these fliers for a wide range of population in your neighborhood. Use your intelligence, initiative and imagination to find out all the possible avenues for mass awareness of the listed requirements for each candidate. Send a copy of each of these fliers to the respective contesting candidates with copies to local television, radio and newspaper media. I am sure that the media will be interested, as they very much care about the rating of their broadcast. Request your candidate and the media to arrange for a public discussion, like town hall meetings, on the issues you documented in your list. Let the discussion be like the presidential debate we know of. Let the media representative take the roll of a moderator. Let the people or the moderator pose the same question to all the candidates (Republican, Democrat, Independent and others) who participate in this healthy and democratic discussion. Listen carefully what each has to say. Ask each candidate to commit in writing what his/her approach would be to resolve each issue and problem that you have listed in your flier. You definitely need this commitment from each candidate since you need to follow it up once he/she gets elected. No more of false verbal promises by the politicians. They have to commit themselves to do what they promise to you. They are accountable to you since they want you to elect them. Take down notes. Now, you have all the inputs you need to decide on who will serve you better in your government. Personally, I prefer Independents since I don't trust any Republican or any Democrat. But, we need to be realistic here. Knowing what the present political system is, we have to decide between the two evils, viz. Republicans and Democrats. So, you be careful, and decide on the lesser of the two evils in line with whatever your expectations and requirements are.

For heaven's sake, decide on a candidate on this basis. Don't blindly believe what they just preach or promise. Carefully select your candidate, as your living conditions for the next few years depend on whom you send to represent you. This careful selection is extremely important for proper functioning of democracy. Here you have to remember a basic fact of life. **If you really want your tomorrow to be better than yesterday, I'm afraid, you have to do something better today.** This process of selection is very important, but relatively easy for you to do. All you need is your determination to act in the interest of your own bright future. I can't emphasize any more than this.

Okay, you have done the selection of your candidate for each level of government. Then, what follows next is every eligible voter MUST make it a point to cast his or her vote. There should be no excuse on this count. It must be done, if you really want your democracy to function properly.

I have detailed to a considerable extent in the sections above in this chapter what each of us, whether we are eligible to vote or not, need to do to ensure that excellent voter turnout is realized. Our aim must be to eliminate poor voter turnout. Only then can our government be reckoned to represent the will of all the people. So, we must ensure that we select the candidates of our choice carefully, and vote for those candidates. Any failure in these two respects will have serious consequences in our present and future way of life.

<u>Step 2</u>:

As briefed before, this step is not that easy since the enemy we face here are the well-established special interests, who have all the determination, resources and backing to continue the current status quo. So, what can you do? You cannot control the special interests. All you can do is to control your elected candidates. How do we do that? In essence, this is what we can do. The people must force each and every one of the elected candidates, top to bottom, to report regularly on their performance and activities. The people should take appropriate punitive action, if need be, to ensure that the elected candidates really do what they were expected and elected to do.
So, as a precondition to select a candidate of your choice, you insist that if a candidate wants your vote he/she must agree and commit in writing to the following:

1. Will not accept any campaign contribution from any special interest, but instead will make appropriate laws to find alternate sources of funds to account for the election expenses.

2. Will not allow any lobbyist to influence the law making process.

3. Will make appropriate laws to find the lobbyist who attempts to contact the elected members of the congress and severely punish that lobbyist when found guilty.

4. Will, every fortnight, report to the people in the respective constituency, using the journals and magazines that are provided to the public free of cost, in every town and village, in respect of every one of their activities and performance as members of the congress:

• The hours they were physically present in the congress to attend to the activities of the law making process.
• Details of their activities in respect of what they did while they did not attend to the proceedings of the congress.

• The details of a law being discussed in the congress explaining how good or bad that law is to the ordinary citizen along with an explanation on how he/she is intending to vote.

• The law that they voted for or against already explaining the reasons for their action including the impact of that law to the ordinary citizen.

5. In addition, will agree to report to the people once a month, through local televised town hall meetings, explaining their performance and activities in the past month.

6. Will agree to arrange for a process of referendum in the respective constituency for the people to decide whether he/she is doing the job to the satisfaction of the people and to resign if people or not satisfied.

7. Will agree for a nationwide referendum for the people to decide whether there should be any salary increase or not to the members of the congress.

8. Will agree to enact a law for a nationwide referendum for the people to decide in the case of major issues like taking the country to a war.

All the stipulations made above are simply in line with the basic concept of the fact that the people are the employers and every legislature is an employee to serve that boss. We, the working citizens, are subjected to this type of scrutiny and performance based reward or punishment everyday in our walk of life. As such, these elected candidates should be viewed and treated exactly in the same manner.

As briefed before, it is not an easy task. Even if we manage to get the prospective candidate to commit to these stipulations, constantly and consistently monitoring these aspects won't be that easy. Because, the special interests have a lot of power and resources to ensure that none, or any of these are really put into effect. If you try to enforce it, they will do their best to stop you from doing that. You may get threatening letters like how the anti-war celebrities had prior to Iraq invasion. I won't be surprised, like how it happened during Florida election in 2000, if Tom Delay's troops are sent to intimidate you for trying to enforce this.

In spite of all these obstacles, please believe me, you can do it because you have to do in the interest of the proper functioning of the democracy. You have to make a difference like how Rosa Parks did on 12/01/1955 in Montgomery, Alabama for Dr. Martin Luther King to pursue and follow it up in a peaceful but powerful way. You have to make a difference like how Mahatma Gandhi did to get rid of the British from India. He did not resort to violence. He did not use a mighty military for this. He, being so humble and simple, used his mighty mental strength for this purpose.

Have you seen the movie "*Gandhi,*" that won so many Oscar awards? In case you haven't seen it yet, please see it. It is an eye opener. I will also encourage you to read "*The Life of Mahatma Gandhi*" by Louis Fischer (1896-1970), an American journalist. Sir Winston Churchill, one of the greatest Prime Ministers of the Great Britain, had the audacity and arrogance to call Gandhi a "half-naked fakir." As per Katherine Frank (Page 182 – "*The Life of Indira Nehru Gandhi*"), Churchill proclaimed, "I have not become the King's first Minister in order to preside over the liquidation of the British Empire." Gandhi did not resort to civil war. He pursued peaceful but powerful means, viz. non-violence and non-cooperation to make British rulers quit India. Martin Luther King met Mr. Gandhi personally to seek Gandhi's advice and guidance for his movement in America.

All I am trying to impress upon each and every one of the readers is just this. You can do it provided you have the will and determination to do it. Of course, you may face with numerous intimidating tactics from the special interests. Don't loose your cool. Be patient, but persistent. Resort to only peaceful non-violent methods to get the country back to the people. Now, we are living in Corporate America. We must do everything we can to live in the United States of America as our founding fathers intended us to do. So, get the country back from the clutches of the corporations. We need to do this for the welfare of our children and grandchildren. Failure in this respect should not be an option for us.

Of course, you can't do it alone. Remember, "united we stand, but divided we fall." So, you have to organise groups of people who believe in similar things to work towards this noble cause. Thanks to Mr. Bush, a lot of people are still desperately looking for decent jobs. Perhaps these people can find some time to become activists to fight for the noble cause of moderate views but definitely not the extremist views in politics or religion. Depending on wherever you are and whatever you do, you can collectively as a dedicated team device ways and means to arrive at appropriate and amicable peaceful and non-violent methods to reach your goal. Please pursue peaceful approach. No violence of any sort even if you are provoked. Your inner strength will be tested numerous times. Don't give up. Like our leaders and legends viz. Mr. Gandhi, Rosa Parks, Dr. King, Nelson Mandela, etc. have mighty mental strength to carry on with your noble mission of getting rid of the injustice inflicted on this nation. Good Luck and God Bless.

Points for *Something to Think About*:

- Democratic government must be of the people, by the people and for the people.
- The responsibilities bestowed on American citizens are far greater than those of the citizens of other countries.
- The most important duty of every citizen is to carefully select and vote for his/her candidate so that the government truly represents the will of the people.
- Effective immediate, it is essential to implement throughout the country a reliable, proven and foolproof electronic voting system that will register and report the data on *"who voted for whom"* accurately and immediately.
- To really represent the will of ALL the people, the Chief Executive Officer of your government must be elected only by the popular votes but not by the electoral votes.
- The present system of political nomination of the Supreme Court Judges, FBI, CIA, FEC, FCC, etc. is corrupt and must be changed. Independent people, with no political affiliation or persuasion, working in the respective system, must make nomination and selection of all the chief candidates. Besides, there should be an appropriate retirement age for the Supreme Court Judges. The concept of job forever, irrespective of their mental state of health as they get older, does not make any sense.
- The duty of the members of the Congress is to make laws, with the consent of the people, to protect and take care of the interests of the people.
- "Corporations have taken over the government and turned it against its own people." - Ralph Nader.

- "I hope we shall crush in its birth, the aristocracy of our moneyed corporations, which dare, already, to challenge our government to a trial of strength and bid defiance to the laws of our country. "- Thomas Jefferson, 3rd US president 1801-1809
- "I see in the near future a crisis approaching that unnerves me and causes me to tremble for the safety of my country...corporations have been enthroned and an era of corruption in high places will follow, and the money of the country will endeavour to prolong its reign by working upon the prejudices of the people until all wealth is aggregated in a few hands and the Republic is destroyed. I feel at this moment more anxiety for the safety of my country than ever before, even in the midst of war." -President Abraham Lincoln
- The corporate share of taxes paid has fallen from 33 percent in the 1940s to 15 percent in the 1990s. Individuals' share of taxes has risen from 44 to 73 percent.
- The chief problem in America is not corrupt people in a good system, but good people in a corrupt system. Our system of government is the problem. We've got to change the system. You could replace everybody in Congress, find the best people in the country, put them in that system, and in months they'd look just like the people you're replacing.
- Immediate steps must be taken to ensure that bribery and bullying by the lobbyists are eliminated forever.
- Immediate steps must be taken to ensure that no candidates receive any sort or form of money from any vested interests.
- Why do the vested interests give campaign contributions to the candidates?
- "All that is necessary for evil to triumph is for good men to do nothing" – Edmund Burke
- "Freedom is the last best hope of earth" - Abraham Lincoln
- "… Our fathers brought forth on this continent a new nation, conceived in liberty and dedicated to the proposition that all men are created equal" - Abraham Lincoln
- "Those who expect to reap the blessings of freedom must, like men, undergo the fatigue of supporting it" – Thomas Paine
- "Ask not what your country can do for you; ask what you can do for your country" – John Kennedy
- "Only our individual faith in freedom can keep us free" – Dwight Eisenhower
- "America is not anything if it consists of each of us. It is something

only if it consists of all of us" – Woodrow Wilson
• Immediate effective measures should be undertaken to take the millions of homeless and starving people off the street.
• Poor voter turnout is the main reason for the failure of democracy.
• Ensure that every eligible voter votes, and every vote counts.
• Do all you can to help, educate, and persuade your neighbours to vote for the candidates of their choice.
• The people must force each elected candidate, top to bottom, to report regularly to the people on his/her performance and activities. The people should take appropriate punitive action, if need be, to ensure that the elected candidates really do what they were expected and elected to do.
• If you really want your tomorrow to be better than yesterday, you have to do something better today.

The Duties of a Citizen

It is my duty to obey my country's laws.
It is my duty to vote, so my government may truly represent the will of the people.
It is my duty to keep informed as to the honesty and ability of candidates for public office.
It is my duty, by my votes and my influence, to correct injustice.
It is my duty to pay such taxes as have been devised by representatives elected by me, to defray the cost of government.
It is my duty to serve on a jury when called on.
It may sometimes become my duty to hold a public office for which I am suited, so my government may function efficiently.
It is my duty to defend my country, if need should arise.
It is my duty to abide by the will of the majority, to stand behind my governments, so my nation may be unified in time of crisis.

Rights and Privileges of a Citizen

I may think as I please.

I may speak or write as I please, so long as I do not interfere with the rights of others.

I have the right to vote. By my vote I choose the public officers who are really my servants.

I have the right to choose my work, to seek any job for which my experience and ability have fitted me.

I have the right to try to improve my lot through various means.

I have the right to prompt a trial by jury, if I should be accused of a crime.

I may seek justice in courts, where I have equal rights with others.

I have the privilege of sharing in the benefits of many of the natural resources of my country.

I may educate my children in free schools.

I have the right to worship as I think best.

I have the right to "life, liberty, and the pursuit of happiness."

The Five Qualities of the Good Citizen

THE GOOD CITIZEN cherishes democratic values and bases his actions on them.

The good citizen gives allegiance to the ideals of democracy. He cherishes values that are consistent with the democratic way of life, and lives in the spirit of these values. He has respect for the dignity and worth of human personality. He has faith in man's ability to solve common problems through the process of thinking. He is concerned with the general welfare of all people; he believes that human culture belongs to all men. He is loyal to the principles of equality of opportunity for all. All other characteristics of the good citizen stem from, and are a part of, this primary quality.

THE GOOD CITIZEN practices democratic human relationship in the family, school, community, and the larger scenes.

The GOOD CITIZEN recognizes the interdependence of all people in family, school, community, national, and world relationships. He practices the kinds of human relationships that are consistent with a democratic society. He personalizes what happens to others, thereby earning respect and confidence.

He develops his own ability to cooperate with others. He sincerely desires to help other persons. Through these practices, he builds good will as resource for the future.

THE GOOD CITIZEN recognizes the social problems of the times and has the will and the ability to work toward their solution.

The GOOD CITIZEN recognizes and endeavours to help in the solution of social problems; problems of race, religion, economics, politics – problems of the role of government in relation to the people; problems of the United States in the place of world affairs; problems of the equitable use of resources; problems of family, school, community, and neighborhood living.

The GOOD CITIZEN is aware of and takes responsibility for meeting basic human needs.

The GOOD CITIZEN is aware of the importance of meeting human needs and is concerned with the extension of the essentials of life to more individuals. All people have certain basic human needs; the need to be free from aggression, domination, or exploitation; the need for love and affection; the need to belong to groups and to be helped by others; the need to take responsibility in cooperation with others; the need for a level of living which provides for adequate health, housing, and recreation; the need to have high standards of spiritual, ethical, and moral values. The failure to meet these fundamental human needs may result in the development of maladjustments which increase the intensity of social problems.

The GOOD CITIZEN possesses and uses knowledge, skills, and abilities necessary in a democratic society.

The GOOD CITIZEN possesses knowledge, skills, and abilities through facility in reading, listening, discussing, and observing. He uses these skills and abilities in order to gain understanding of the present structure and functioning of society, the working principles of representative government, the impact of pressure groups, the operation of the economic system, the social satisfaction of the population, and the relationship of all these to the complex social heritage. With knowledge, skills, and abilities as a basis, the good citizen becomes more proficient in civic action.

<u>Draft of a possible brief note to the neighbours</u>

Dear Neighbour,

I live here in this community. My contact information is given below. Please spare just a few moments.

<u>This note is for every registered voter in your family.</u>

Let us please have an excellent voter turnout from our community. I am contacting you only for this reason.

Is everything okay and ready for you to vote?

Please check again and make sure that you are registered to vote. Don't assume.

Come what may, will you definitely vote?
If your answer is "**YES**," then my reply is "**THANKS**." However, please let me know, if you need *__any__* help in this respect. Please, please VOTE.

If your answer is "**Not Sure**" or "**NO**," then my reply is "**is there anything, anything at all, I can do to help you to vote?** Every vote is extremely important. **Your vote may prove to be the deciding vote**. We never know. Please, please VOTE. Please contact me. I will do all I can to help you to vote. Thanks.

First Name:
Last Name:
Phone Number:
E-mail:
Address:

What I want my candidate to promise to do for me?

These are just some samples. Requirements vary as appropriate for local, state and federal level candidates because of the limitations on what they can do in the respective level. Most of these are appropriate for the heads of each level viz. President, Governor and Mayor as well.

If a candidate wants my vote then, as a precondition, must agree and commit in writing to the following:

1. Will not accept any campaign contribution from any special interest, but instead will make appropriate laws to find alternate source of funds to account for the election expenses.

2. Will not allow any lobbyist to influence the law making process.

3. Will make appropriate laws to find and punish the lobbyist and the elected member who are found guilty of corruption and favoritism in the law making process.

4. Every fortnight will report to the people for whom the elected member is responsible. The journals and magazines that are available in every town and village free of cost to the public can be used in this respect. The report should be on their activities and performance as members of the congress viz.

• The hours they were physically present in the congress to attend to the proceedings of the congress.
• Explanation for not attending the proceedings, if it so happens.
• The details of a law presently being discussed in the congress explaining how good or bad that law is to the ordinary citizen along with an explanation on how he/she is intending to vote.
• The details of the law that they already voted for or against along with the reasons for their action including the impact of that law to the ordinary citizen.

5. In addition, will agree to report to the people once a month, through local televised town hall meetings, explaining their performance and activities in the past month.

6. Will agree to arrange for a process of referendum for the people to decide whether he/she is doing the job to the satisfaction of the people concerned and to resign if people or not satisfied.

7. Will agree to enact a law for a nationwide referendum for the people to decide on major issues like taking the country to a war and on any pay raise to the members of the congress.

8. Will agree to enact appropriate laws that will protect and take care of the interests of every citizen, especially the homeless, starving and low-income group of citizens. For example, the laws should cover the following concepts:
• The homeless and starving people must be taken off the street, provided with some sort of basic food and shelter and forced to do whatever work they can in return for the food and shelter they get.
• Decent jobs where we can use our whatever skills we may have, education, experience and expertise to earn enough income to have a roof over us, food to eat, educate our children and pay the bills.
• Decent habitable home, preferably own it, in a safe and secured environment where we don't have to worry about robbery, mugging, thieving and murder.
• Well-established educational system, schools and support to prepare the future citizens of our country as loving, caring and sharing type.
• Excellent educational opportunities must not be confined just to the rich only but must be available to all to access.
• Universal healthcare system for **ALL**.
• To avoid conflict of interest, every state should assign all the responsibilities associated with the election process to a civil servant who is independent and free from any political bias.
• A reliable, proven and foolproof electronic voting system to register and report accurately and immediately the data on "who voted for whom" must be implemented in every state effective immediate.

• Media prediction of the election results must be delayed until all the votes are cast in all the states including Hawaii since earlier prediction unduly influences the voters in the west.

• The Chief Executive Officer, viz. the President of the democratic government must represent the will of ALL the people. So, the President must be elected by the popular votes and NOT by the electoral votes.

• The Judiciary system should function free from any political influence. So, the present practice of political nomination of judges should be stopped. The members of the Judiciary System must decide on the appointment of judges.

• All the loopholes that enable the corporations to avoid paying due taxes must be closed and all the tax evaders must be severely punished.

• Protect the people from the local terrorists, viz. gangs, robbers, rapists, etc. Constantly monitor the movements of the known offenders. Round up the offender immediately on the first act of violence and keep them in boot camps until such time these offenders are rehabilitated as acceptable citizens of the community.

War on Terror

At the outset, I would very much like to convey our heartfelt deep sense of gratitude and respect to our young men and women, fire fighters, and law enforcing personnel, who are facing danger every minute when they are out at work. These brave men and women are risking their lives every day. Just imagine the sacrifice they are making. Every morning when they start their work, they are not sure whether they will get back home to see their loved ones. So, we salute them and thank them for what they do. We are ever so grateful to these brave people who work so hard for our safe living. THANKS. God bless you all.

The whole world is talking about the "War on Terror" these days. Let us try and look at it with an open mind like any ordinary concerned citizen would or should, but not like politicians, and find answers for the following simple basic questions:

1. Who are these terrorists?
2. Why do they do what they do?
3. What can we do, individually and collectively, to contain it initially and stop it eventually?

The present preaching by the politicians against terrorism is that the terrorists are the followers of Osama bin Laden, Saddam Hussein, and the Islamic fundamentalists. The main reason for their atrocities are to destroy the Western free, democratic, and civilized way of life.

If we really want to resolve any serious problem, we have to be really sincere to find out what the real reasons are for that problem. No point in just being blind in this respect since this is anything but plain stupidity. So, as for *"Why the West is Losing the War on Terror,"* please check out the real reasons presented by *"Anonymous"* who devoted 17 years to track Al Qaeda and other terrorists in his book *"Imperial Hubris."*

Before we analyse this issue in detail, let us look at the following local issues first:

- Do you feel relaxed and safe staying at your own residence?
- Do you feel relaxed and safe, especially if you are a woman, to go out alone for a walk or shopping at night?

I am sure that the answer is "NO." Then, the question is "WHY NOT?" Yes, you are worried about getting attacked by burglars, robbers, rapists, gang members, etc. These are our local terrorists, who are just around some of you in your own neighborhood. Your existence is threatened in your own neighborhood. In many areas, cars that are parked outside overnight on the drive way are not to be seen the following morning.

Why are the lawmakers and law enforcers not taking this issue seriously and do something positive to eliminate this local terror? These thugs are not hiding in caves or in the woods. They are living and moving around in your own neighborhood. Police personnel have records on most of these thugs. How would you feel and react, if you were attacked, or raped, or had your property burgled by any of these thugs? How would you feel when you hear that one of your neighbors, who went out to the corner shop, did not return home? How would you feel when you hear the stories about the innocent victims who happened to be at the wrong place at the wrong time when the gang fights started suddenly? Do you think that it won't happen to you? You don't have to wait too long. It is just a matter of time. The expensive burglar alarm set up at your residence may give you some sort of false feeling of safety, provided you stay put at your home at all time. Do you want to do that?

As for, "why do they do, what they do," the blame goes on the respective parents and the society these thugs live in. We will checkout the details on this in "The Marriage and Family Life" and "Violence" chapters.

So, what can we do?

You may know, or know of, these terrorists who live in your community. He/she may be your neighbor, your own son/daughter, or brother/sister, or co-worker. Then, if you really care about that person and the people around you, why don't you have a real good detailed discussion with that person explaining the eventual consequences of his/her criminal acts?

The chances are, that person may not listen to your advice, whatever be the reason, and change his/her behavior. In that case, in the interest of everyone around you, especially that person, why don't you consider the following remedial course of actions?

• Give an ultimatum to that person to the effect that, if he/she refuses to stop the criminal activities, you would contact the local police. If there is no change, then do contact the police. I realize that it is easier said than done. You may get intimidated and threatened. But, what is the alternative? If you don't do anything positive to stop this, then your neighbor, or even you may be the next victim, and the offender eventually will get rounded up for serious crime and even may get shot or killed. Sure, you don't want this to happen to anyone in your community. So, please do something positive in the interest of all concerned.

• Contact your local, state and federal lawmakers insisting that appropriate legislative action must be effected immediately to minimize and eventually eliminate this problem for good. Presently the laws seem to be more lenient towards the offenders. What happened to the innocent victim's right? Shouldn't that be our primary concern? While I was working in Saudi Arabia, we never had to experience this type of fear. The criminals know very well what the outcome would be when they are caught. Yes, it is true. The Saudi laws may seem primitive and barbaric. But, it really works as an excellent deterrent. Innocent people must be saved and protected at all cost. Request your lawmakers and government officials to explore and implement laws that will

1. Monitor the movement of the known offenders, as a preventive measure,
2. Round up the offender on the first act of violence, and
3. Send them to the boot camps (Correctional facilities that use the training techniques applied to military recruits to teach the offenders socially acceptable patterns of behaviors) and keep them there until such time these offenders are rehabilitated as caring citizens acceptable to the community.

I am positive we will get the usual story saying that they haven't got

enough resources to fund for more law enforcing personnel, jails, boot camps, etc. Then, tell those guys whose main responsibility is to provide protection for us to find resources immediately. <u>What is more important than our right to live in our own community free from the fear of robbery, rape, vandalism, murder, gang violence, drive by shootings, etc.?</u> Be a real pain in the back to your law makers and government officials, and insist that they have to get this issue as one of their top most priority items that needs to be successfully resolved at the earliest possible time. We can't wait any more. Life is short. We don't know what is in store for us the next minute. We have the right to live peacefully in our own community. It is not too much to ask for.

Please use your conscience and common sense to consider the cited suggestions seriously. Take positive actions as appropriate for your community. If you really wish to lead a normal and peaceful life in your own neighbourhood, then this is not something to ignore. You need to constantly pester your local lawmakers and government officials until a working solution is found for this serious menace in your community. Anyway, the ball is in your court and it is your life we are talking about. So, you need to do something now but not at a later date. Because, in big cities like Chicago, New York. Los Angeles, etc., the chances are that you may not get to see that later date.

Having talked about the local terrorists, now let us concentrate on the foreign terrorists.

Now, since just prior to Iraq invasion US Administration accused Saddam as a terrorist, let us talk about the recent Iraq invasion and occupation.

Prior to going into the details on this subject, I request the readers to ask the warmongers in the Bush Administration to answer to this real simple question.

Out of all those brave men and women in Iraq, already killed or seriously wounded, or who are still out there, or going there, risking their lives every minute waiting to be killed or seriously wounded, how many are the close family members and friends of those warmongers?

This is just a real simple and fair question. Please find out what they have to say. If I am not mistaken, the answer will be next to nothing. So, why should they worry that much about those soldiers? The body bag is not being delivered to their homes. They don't have to take care of any seriously wounded soldier who is incapacitated for his/her life.

Also, please note, most of these soldiers are from the middle or low-income group families, but not from the families of their rich buddies. When did any right wing administration worry about the working class people? Do they know what it is like for the family members to send their loved ones to the war, especially of late, when they know very well that the chances are they may not see that person alive again. The warmongers care about themselves and their political agenda first and then their rich buddies. This is the fact of life, whether anyone wants to admit or not.

Have you witnessed the physical and emotional reunion of the families and friends when the soldiers, National Guards and Reservists return home after their term of duties in Iraq?

It is true, these soldiers, National Guards and Reservists know very well the risk they undertake, when they joined to serve the country. But, the point I am trying to make here is this. If they were sent out to protect our country and our freedom, when subjected to real imminent or actual attack, then it is okay. But, my blood boils when we know for certain that they were sent out as pawns to get killed or seriously wounded just to fulfil the warmongers' political agenda to dominate the world and control the oil fields in the Middle East.

How about the recent episode in respect of the prisoner abuse scandal in Iraq? Now, the Bush Administration wants us to believe that it is just a few bad apples that did those atrocities on their own, and higher ups have nothing to do with it. Are we that thick to believe this? If those few bad apples want to get some thrill out of torturing the prisoners, without the knowledge of their higher ups, will they pose happily with thumbs up for the photographs and allow videos taken knowing very well that they will be in deep trouble if they are caught? Through those photos, those bad apples want to prove to their superiors that they are doing a real good job as directed to do. Perhaps they were hoping for some sort of promotion for having done the job well as per the directives. But, when everything got leaked out to the public, the administration puts the blame on these poor soldiers who just followed the orders. I am convinced, if and only if, a thorough independent investigation is carried out without any cover up, it is just a matter of time the world will know that these atrocities were authorized from higher ups in the Pentagon.

Let us try and find some answers to the following questions:

- Who created and nurtured the monster Saddam Hussein and why?
- Did Saddam pose any imminent threat to the USA just prior to the recent invasion?
- Was Iraq invasion well planned by Bush Administration even before September 11 attack?
- What was the real reason for invading Iraq now?
- Why do the majority of the world population oppose this Iraq invasion while they supported the previous Gulf war and the efforts to get rid of the followers of Osama bin Laden?
- Who benefits out of the recent Iraq invasion and occupation?

Who created and nurtured the monster Saddam Hussein and why?

Here, we need to look at what was going on between the West, especially US Administration, and Saddam in the 1980s.

Checkout *http://www.consortiumnews.com/2003/022703a.html*. This site gives a real insight into *"Missing U.S.- Iraq History,"* and how Saddam was nurtured during the Presidency periods of Jimmy Carter, Ronald Reagan, and George H. Bush. I show below a few excerpts from this report for you to think about.

- "Both [Egypt's Anwar] Sadat and [then-Saudi Prince] Fahd [explained that] Iran is receiving military spares for U.S. equipment from Israel," Haig noted. "It was also interesting to confirm that President Carter gave the Iraqis a green light to launch the war against Iran through Fahd."
- "When Iran appeared to be winning in 1982, Reagan and his advisers made a fateful decision to secretly supply Saddam's military, including permitting shipments of dual-use technology that Iraq then used to build chemical and biological weapons. Tactical military assistance also was provided, including satellite photos of the battlefield."

• "Last September, for example, *Newsweek* reported that the Reagan administration in the 1980s had allowed sales to Iraq of computer databases, that Saddam could use to track political opponents and shipments of "bacteria/fungi/protozoa," that could help produce anthrax and other biological weapons. [*Newsweek* issue dated Sept. 23, 2002]"

• "Waas and Unger described the motive for the Reagan administration's tactical advice as a kind of diplomatic billiard shot. By getting Iraq to expand use of its air force, the Iranians would be more desperate for U.S.-made HAWK anti-aircraft missile parts, giving Washington more leverage with the Iranians. Iran's need to protect their cities from Iraqi air attacks gave impetus to the Reagan administration's arms-for-hostage scheme, which later became known as the Iran-contra affair. [See The New Yorker, Nov. 2, 1992.]"

• "Before attacking Kuwait, however, Saddam consulted George H.W. Bush's administration. First, the U.S. State Department informed Saddam that Washington had "no special defense or security commitments to Kuwait." Then, U.S. Ambassador April Glaspie told Saddam, "we have no opinion on the Arab-Arab conflicts, like your border disagreement with Kuwait.""

• "Democratic sources say Clinton heeded personal appeals from the elder Bush and other top Republicans to close the books on the so-called "Irangate" investigation – as well as probes into secret Reagan-Bush dealings with Iran – soon after Clinton defeated Bush in the 1992 election."

• "In 1986, President Reagan sent a secret message to Saddam Hussein telling him that Iraq should step up its air war and bombing of Iran," Teicher wrote. "This message was delivered by Vice President Bush who communicated it to Egyptian President Mubarak, who in turn passed the message to Saddam Hussein."

These are just a few to quote for your attention. Besides, Mr. Bush is blaming Saddam now for using chemical and biological weapons on his neighbours. But, look what happened in the previous Republican Administration.

As per Document 47 in *http://www.gwu.edu/~nsarchiv/NSAEBB/ NSAEBB82/,* "The State Department instructs the U.S. delegate to the United Nations to get the support of other Western missions for a motion of "no decision" regarding Iran's draft resolution condemning Iraq's use of chemical weapons. Failing that, the U.S. is to abstain on the resolution."

Besides, please checkout the following also:

• "Document 36: United States Interests Section in Iraq Cable from William L. Eagleton, Jr. to the Department of State. "Meeting With Tariq Aziz: Expanding Iraq's Oil Export Facilities," January 3, 1984.

• During a meeting following Donald Rumsfeld's talks, Tariq Aziz tells William Eagleton that President Saddam Hussein was pleased with the visit and with the positive atmosphere it created. - Source: Declassified under the Freedom of Information Act"

Let me summarize, The West, in particular the USA, created and nurtured that monster Saddam. Why did US Administration do that? He was a real good boy then. He listened to the US Administration to keep Iran under control. Besides, US policy helped to export all types of products from the US, including weapons of mass destruction, to both Iraq and Iran. Yes, supply to both the parties to fight against each other. It is another noble way of making more money. Don't you think?

Now, would you blame me when I say I feel sick to talk about these dirty politicians?

Did Saddam Hussein pose imminent threat to the USA prior to the recent invasion?

The answer is an emphatic "NO."

Please checkout these websites:

As per, *http://www.whodies.com/lies.html*, "The Bush administration has repeatedly lied about Iraq's nuclear, chemical and biological weapons capabilities, as well as lying about Iraq's links with al-Qaeda. The administration has pressured its own analysts to bias evidence toward its war plans, and has not co-operated with UN inspectors."

For the latest, as of 2004/06/17, on this subject please check out *http:// breaking.tcm.ie/2004/06/17/story152692.html* where "9/11 Commission rules out Saddam/al-Qaida link 17/06/2004 - 07:07:47."
As per this site,

"US president George Bush's much-questioned justification for the Iraq war suffered another major setback when an independent commission dismissed claims of a link between Saddam Hussein and al-Qaeda.

The findings of the commission, investigating the September 11, 2001 attacks, comes on top of the Bush administration's failure to find any weapons of mass destruction in Iraq.

Both ideas had been central ingredients of Bush's rationale for invading."

Besides, please checkout the website, *http://www.truthaboutwar.org/ home.shtml*, to find out about "*A History of Lies.*"

In brief, NO evidence existed before the invasion. Even Mr. Bush and Mr. Blair had to reluctantly admit now. As such, there is no real need to provide any more evidence to this effect. The entire world knows that the warmongers have been lying about this all along.

Was the Iraq invasion well planned by Bush Administration even before the September 11 attack?

You bet it was. Please checkout *http://cryptome.org/rad.htm* for full details. Also please checkout *http://oldamericancentury.org/iraq.htm* for the "Archives" on Iraq.

Please checkout the following extract of the text from *www.abcnews.go.com/sections/nightline/DailyNews/pnac_030310.html*

"The group, the Project for the New American Century, or PNAC, was founded in 1997. Among its supporters were three Republican former officials who were sitting out the Democratic presidency of Bill Clinton: Donald Rumsfeld, Dick Cheney, and Paul Wolfowitz.
In open letters to Clinton and GOP congressional leaders the next year,

the group called for "the removal of Saddam Hussein's regime from power," and a shift toward a more assertive U.S. policy in the Middle East, including the use of force if necessary to unseat Saddam.

And in a report just before the 2000 election that would bring Bush to power, the group predicted that the shift would come about slowly, unless there were "some catastrophic and catalyzing event, like a new Pearl Harbor."

That event came on Sept. 11, 2001. By that time, Cheney was vice president, Rumsfeld was secretary of defense, and Wolfowitz his deputy at the Pentagon.

The next morning — before it was even clear who was behind the attacks — Rumsfeld insisted at a Cabinet meeting that Saddam's Iraq should be "a principal target of the first round of terrorism," according to Bob Woodward's book Bush At War.

What started as a theory in 1997 was now on its way to becoming official U.S. foreign policy."
For the contents of the actual open letter dated 01/26/98, checkout *http://www.newamericancentury.org/iraqclintonletter.htm*

As per, *http://www.cbsnews.com/stories/2004/03/19/60minutes/printable607356.shtml*, the latest on *"Did Bush Press For Iraq-9/11 Link?"* comes from the advisor, Richard Clarke, in an exclusive interview on *60 Minutes* dated March 21, 2004.

Every American voter should check out the details of this interview.
So, I have copied some essential excerpts of this interview (*"Did Bush Press For Iraq-9/11 Link?"*) at the end of this chapter.

Further, please checkout the statement of Mr. Bush's former Treasury Secretary Mr. Paul O'Neill in this respect. As per the website, *http://www.cbsnews.com/stories/2004/01/09/60minutes/main592330.shtml*, "From the very beginning, there was a conviction, that Saddam Hussein was a bad person and that he needed to go," says O'Neill, who adds that going after Saddam was topic "A" 10 days after the inauguration - eight months before Sept. 11."
Should I go any further to substantiate this fact? I don't think so. It was

well planned way ahead in advance.

What was the real reason for invading Iraq now?

Is it not obvious yet? It is all part of the big plan, viz. Oil and American global domination. Iraq invasion is just a tiny piece of that big pie.

Please checkout the contents of some of the articles given at the end of this chapter. They are eye openers and every American voter must be aware of them.

It contains two articles. The contents of the 1st article "PNAC Seeks Global Domination" by Shirley Howland is from *http:// www.bulletinboardforpeace.org/articlehowland.htm*

The contents of the 2nd article "US Plan for Global Domination Tops Project Censored's Annual List" by Kari Lydersen is from *http://www.alternet.org/story.html?StoryID=16784.*

The last paragraph of the 1st article states as follows:

"Americans have to decide whether or not they want to rule the world, at a price of trillions of dollars, and countless lives; whether or not they want the nuclear holocaust that is bound to follow this government's attempt at Empire! The military and financial objectives of the PNAC are well on their way to being met as most Americans stand silently by, wave their flags, and pay their taxes."

Also, please checkout this site as well: *http://globalresearch.ca/articles/CHO312A.html*

There are numerous source materials available on the Internet to document the facts on *"American Global Domination."* When a search was made with the cited keywords, the Google Search provided 298,000 links on this topic. Obviously, we cannot bring out all those details herein. But, the proof is there to educate us on American Global Domination.

Why do the majority of the world population oppose this Iraq invasion

while they supported the previous Gulf war and the efforts to get rid of the followers of Osama bin Laden?

There are numerous reasons for this.

First of all, they are better informed than Americans. The foreign media need not have to worry about any pressure from the right wing American administration. As such, they present the facts, without any fabrication, better than American media. The US corporations control American media. It has been reported that they get quite a number of government contracts.

Do you remember the legend journalist Peter Arnett who won wide recognition for his journalistic stature during Vietnam War and Gulf War? As per, *http://news.bbc.co.uk/2/hi/americas/2903503.stm,*

"Iraqi television broadcast him saying 'the first war plan has just failed because of Iraqi resistance. Clearly the American war planners misjudged the determination of the Iraqi forces.'"

He was fired by the NBC for making these statements. He was telling the truth, for heaven sake. He gets fired because he was politically incorrect in his reporting? But, he was correct, as a matter of fact, in his on the spot assessment and presenting those facts as a journalist.

Besides, as per, http://www.us-democratorship.com/links.htm,

"A completely different view on the Iraq war. ABC, CBS, NBC, CNN and Fox News are all competing to get the largest market share in the USA by presenting a "comfortable" view on the war, that the typical American patriot wants to see during his breakfast or lunch hour, or as his "evening entertainment." Fox News is probably the most "patriotic" of those News services. For Europeans like me often disgusting to see, but unfortunately reality. This is modern war propaganda in the year 2003. They spoon-feed America with all the thin arguments the Bush administration could find to justify this war."

Then, whether you like to admit or not, the fact is, the rest of the world is not that materialistic like Americans. Most of us here in the USA are selfish, and have no concern for the well being of other human beings. All we care about is "I come first, and what is in it for me?" When Iraq invaded and occupied Kuwait, most of the world population rallied behind America during Gulf war. Likewise, they are giving the same type of support to get rid of the followers of Bin Laden. But, now the story is entirely different with the Iraq invasion by the Bush Administration. Unlike most of the Americans who still continue to be blind in this context, the rest of the world can see what Bush Administration is up to with the Iraq invasion and occupation. So, obviously, they don't give their support now.

Besides, they have no regard or respect for Mr. Bush. They don't trust him. Because, they are aware of how he got to the white house. What a shame? In spite of him being the "compassionate conservative," and the controller of a super power, he is unable to win the hearts of the rest of the world like how Mr. Kennedy and Mr. Clinton did. I don't blame them. In spite of the alleged personal weaknesses of these two former Presidents, the world did respect them because these two former Presidents, unlike Mr. Bush, cared for everyone, in particular the working class people.

Another point to note here is this: most of the citizens of the rest of the world don't just follow the bandwagon like how Americans do in the name of patriotism. They use their head. They are not biased. When Kuwait was attacked, they rallied behind America. When twin towers were attacked, they rallied behind America. Why? Because, they witnessed the injustice inflicted on the innocent people of Kuwait and the USA. For the same reason, now they do **NOT** rally behind America. They witness the injustice being inflicted on the innocent Iraqi civilians now. They see the American Global Domination and the American greed for the oil in the Middle East. They do not agree with Bush Administration's hidden agenda of blood for oil and world domination.

Do you recall the resistance made in the UN by Russia, China, Germany, France, etc., etc., refusing to give UN's okay signal to the USA to invade Iraq? They wanted the weapons inspectors to complete their jobs. I'm not saying that the heads of these countries are angels either. Of course, they do have their own vested interests. They are politicians. What do you expect from any politician? Anyway, what did the US Administration and Media do? They accused all these countries, especially France, for not yielding to Bush's pressure.

What did our American "patriots" do? They hated anything and everything to do with France. They poured the French wine that they loved dearly down the drain. They boycotted the French restaurants. They cancelled their vacation to France. They renamed French fries as Freedom fries. Forget about the mass for a moment. They very rarely use their head, but instead the bandwagon approach by the name of patriotism carries them away.

How about our illustrious Members of the Congress? We expect them to be mentally more matured and balanced. We expect them to reason out and respond to any situation based on facts, but not on prejudice. What did they do? They too joined the bandwagon and changed the name of French fries as Freedom fries in their dining menu. Why did they do that? Obviously they did not want the so-called "patriots" to think of them as unpatriotic. As a principle, can't they stand up and fight for what they believe in? NO, because they are politicians and they don't want to be unpopular in the eyes of the "patriots." As per the constitution, the congress only can declare the war. But, what did really happen? Bush declares the war and these gutless members of the congress back him up with their votes. Why? They are thinking of their present popularity and the next election. Isn't it pathetic?

When the original colonies of America wanted to break away from Britain, who helped the colonies to defeat British army? It was France.

Who gave the Statue of Liberty as a gift to the USA? It was the French people.

As per, *http://whc.unesco.org/sites/307.htm,* the Statue of Liberty was "made in Paris by the French sculptor Bartholdi, in collaboration with Gustave Eiffel (who was responsible for the steel framework), this towering monument to liberty was a gift from France on the centenary of American independence in 1886."

Besides, as per the website,
http://www.info-france-usa.org/franceus/history/exch4.asp,
"Money for the statue itself came from a generous subscription fund in France and its pedestal was financed by the United States."

Who was the first foreign head of state to visit Washington D.C.

immediately after 9/11 to offer his support and condolences to the people of this great nation? It was the French President.

Who was leading the UN Security Council process, the day after 9/11, condemning the attacks and demanding justice for the innocent victims? It was the French team.

Didn't our so-called "patriots" and our legislatures behave really silly and mean in this context?

By the way, the warmongers are not the patriots. The people who refused to use their head but instead blindly believed the warmongers' propaganda are not the patriots. The members of the Congress who had no guts to stand up and fight for what they believe in are not the patriots.

The people who opposed this unjustifiable Iraq invasion and occupation are the real patriots. You know why? These people really do care about the well being of our soldiers, soldiers' families and the innocent Iraqi civilians. These people do not want our young men and women and the Iraqi innocent civilians to shed their blood or die in exchange for oil and American Global domination. These people are the real patriots, whether you want to admit or not. You, the warmongers and the so-called patriots are really responsible for all the ever-increasing deaths in Iraq and the US national debt. You can't wipe away the blood you've got on your hands now. I sincerely hope that God will forgive you for your ignorance.

It was purely pathetic when Mr. Bush, during his "State of the Union" speech, was citing the names of those countries that are part of the so-called "coalition of the willing." That shows his confidence in fooling the people. Are we that stupid? Our neighbors, Canada and Mexico, did not want to be part of these American atrocities. Do you remember the pestering and bullying Mr. Collin Powell did to get the final UN Security Council Members' votes prior to Iraq invasion? In spite of his persistent pressure, he couldn't get enough support from the members to get his resolution passed by the Security Council. The heads of those countries that refused to join American atrocities do have conscience. They can clearly see the right from wrong.

Okay, the Bush Administration managed to persuade quite a few countries to join in return for some sort of favor by Bush Administration and / or the threat of "join us or else." Except for the contribution by Britain, as we all know very well, effective and substantial contributions by these so-called "coalition of the willing" are next to nothing. The whole world knows that it is just two crazy men's show, viz. Bush and Blair.

Having lived and worked in the United Kingdom for quite a while, I find it extremely hard to believe that Mr. Blair, the most popular leader of a labor movement, would join Bush in this unjustifiable adventure. I still believe that he is a loving and caring family man. He is not an extremist on either side of the political spectrum. He is just another "middle of the road" guy like most of us. I may be wrong. But, honestly, I still believe that he will do his best to take care of the interests of the working class people.

But, why on earth did he join this right wing extremist, Mr. Bush, to invade Iraq and continue supporting him? It is a real big puzzle to my comprehension. I can think of just one or two reasons. Mr. Blair is a very sharp, smart and shrewd politician. Perhaps, he is fully aware of the consequences, if he refuses to join Bush in this respect.

The British Empire is not there anymore. But, still there are a few small spots around the world in far away places as British colonies or territories. Remember the Falklands War in early 1980s, during Thatcher and Reagan period? Britain won that war largely because of considerable help from the USA. We never know, there may be similar occasions in future also and Britain would definitely need the help from the "super power" to take care of British interests.

Perhaps, it may be the fear of trade sanctions and embargo by the US Administration. May be, being a politician, in view of the overall national interest, he cannot confess these facts to the British people.

We never know. But, one thing is certain. He failed the British people. He betrayed their trust. In spite of the massive opposition by the British people to this Iraq invasion, he joined Bush and took Britain to war.

No loving and caring citizens of the Great Britain could forgive Mr. Blair for what he has done. This is time for all the caring British citizens to prove once again to the world that these dirty politicians cannot take you for a ride all the time. Mr. Blair must be punished for what he has done against the will of the people. Previously you provided landslide victory to Mr. Blair. He doesn't deserve it anymore. Luckily in the United Kingdom, you have a third party, Liberal Democrat, who hopefully will take care of the interests of the ordinary working class people. Perhaps, it is time to check them out by giving a landslide victory to this third party. Should this happen, the arrogance of the other two parties will be kept on hold for quite a while.

So, I appeal to each and every one of the caring British citizens with this message. Most of you, the caring British people, are not like most of the American "middle of the road" people. You guys think properly and you are not materialistic like most of the Americans. For you guys, the money is important, but not everything. You respect the human values better than Americans. It is time again for you British people to shock the entire world again with another landslide victory, this time with the Liberal Democrats. We never know. The Liberal Democrats may turn out to be the caring type of people. It is worth trying them out. Definitely, it won't get any worse than what it is right now. By providing another landslide victory, you will tell and teach the world to the effect that you have the power and you are the boss when it comes to running your government. You have done it before and you need to do it again. Please carefully think this through and do something really positive in the interest of the hard working citizens of the Great Britain.

Who benefits out of the recent Iraq invasion and occupation?

It is a real bright idea by the Bush Administration. You want to grab oil and dominate the world. So, as a start, go and bomb Iraq and wipe off almost all the infrastructure in that country. So, there comes the need for re-building Iraq. While the rest of the world population is grieving over the entire episode, all the big corporations in the world are queuing up and bribing the people concerned to secure the multimillion-dollars rebuilding Iraq contracts. Who is paying for the war and the re-building? It will be none other than we, the American taxpayers.

Okay, who are the real beneficiaries of these re-building contracts award? As per the website, http://www.opensecrets.org/news/rebuilding_iraq/index.asp,

"Even before the war in Iraq began March 20, the Bush administration

81

was considering plans to help rebuild the country after fighting ceased. According to news reports in early March, the U.S. Agency for International Development secretly asked six U.S. companies to submit bids for a $900 million government contract to repair and reconstruct water systems, roads, bridges, schools and hospitals in Iraq.

The six companies -- Bechtel Group Inc., Fluor Corp., Halliburton Co. subsidiary Kellogg, Brown & Root, Louis Berger Group Inc., Parsons Corp. and Washington Group International Inc. -- contributed a combined $3.6 million in individual, PAC and soft money donations between 1999 and 2002, *The Center* reported on its news site, CapitalEye.org. Sixty-six percent of that total went to Republicans. "

Please don't forget this: $900 million contracts are just the starters. Still there are plenty to grab as long as the contractors are nice to the Bush Administration. Please also note that it is a secret deal between USAID and six campaign contributors of their choice. Perhaps, "name your price and you got it" was the name of the game here. Who knows? Normally in any contract business, at least three competitive quotes would be required to select the best bidder. But, there was no need for that in this case. Perhaps no other companies in this planet earth can do the jobs that these six companies are asked to do. It is not Mr. Bush, but it is the taxpayers paying the bill. So, why should Mr. Bush worry about it, I guess?

The site *http://www.usaid.gov/iraq/activities.html* provides the details of the contracts.

Definitely tax-paying citizens are not the beneficiaries. The beneficiaries are the big corporations who have been generous to the Republicans.

Of course, the atrocities of Osama bin Laden and his followers started the war in Afghanistan. On top of this, owing to Mr. Bush's unwritten obligation to his rich buddies, those millionaires and billionaires were blessed with massive tax cuts. Then comes the unnecessary and unjustified Iraq invasion and occupation. As such, our national debt keeps rising all the time. Who is going to pay for all these national debts? Obviously, besides you and me, it will be our children and grandchildren eventually. They have to work ever so hard to pay back this debt.

One final note on this Iraq issue:

Okay, Mr. Bush, you lied so much by way of justification to invade Iraq. Unfortunately for you, of late, everyone is aware of all your lies. Now, you started saying that you catalyzed this regime change because the world is a better place without Saddam in power anymore. What a great savior you are! You are the living form of God whom any human can see since you saved the world from Saddam. You are a true noble and compassionate conservative. You proved it.

Now that you saved the world, why don't you and your buddy Blair pack up your bags and get back. Leave the Iraq's stability and re-building issues to the United Nations Administration. It is their responsibility. That is why the UN was formed to start of. **We find more and more violence in Iraq now because they do not want American and British occupation anymore in their land. The moment you leave and the UN takes over the remaining issues, the violence will drop dramatically.** If you are truly interested in peace in that region and have any concern for the ever-increasing American national debt, this is what you should do. Just pack up and get back. The locals will co-operate well with the UN members in their effort to get their country back to peace and prosperity. **All the Iraqis want now is for you to leave Iraq for good, NOW.**

But, everybody knows very well that you won't leave Iraq. **You invaded Iraq for oil and global domination at the expense of so many lives in Iraq and enormous national debt here.** Please for your own sake don't keep on lying. The entire world is now fully aware of your credibility gap.

Now, let us talk about the foreign terrorists who inflicted serious damage on September 11, 2001.

First of all, let me state the following:

• I do not believe that there is any religion that suggests or instigates or induces violence or killing. But, I do believe that it is all due to the deliberate wrong interpretation by the preachers or the followers to suit their vested interests. But, if really there is any such religion, I don't want to know about it.

• The despicable acts of Osama bin Laden and his followers deserve nothing but contempt and condemnation.

Who are these terrorists, and why do they do, what they do?

The answers to these two questions are well answered in the website, *http://www.cnn.com/SPECIALS/2001/gulf.war/legacy/bin.laden/.*

The full text version of the contents of this site is given at the end of this chapter (*An elusive enemy*). The readers are urged to read this to get a real picture and understanding on why Osama bin Laden is hell bent on instigating all these atrocities on Americans.

These terrorists are religious fundamentalists and extremists like Bin Laden and his followers.

Here are a few excerpts on some of the salient points.

"His rage stems from the decision by Saudi Arabia to allow the United States to use the country as a staging area for attacks on Iraqi forces in Kuwait and Iraq. After the victory, the U.S. military presence became permanent."

"To fundamentalists like bin Laden, the U.S. presence is anathema because Saudi Arabia is home to 'the two most holy places' in Islam -- Mecca and Medina."

"In an interview bin Laden gave to CNN in 1997, he said the ongoing U.S. military presence in Saudi Arabia is an 'occupation of the land of the holy places.'"

"In February 1998, bin Laden issued a "fatwa," a religious ruling, calling for Muslims to kill Americans and their allies. Three other groups, including the Islamic Jihad in Egypt, endorse the ruling."

"The ruling to kill the Americans and their allies - civilians and military - is an individual duty for every Muslim who can do it, in any country in which it is possible to do it, in order to liberate the al-Aqsa Mosque and the holy mosque from their grip, and in order for American armies to move out of all the lands of Islam, defeated and unable to threaten any Muslim," the statement was issued under the name"World Islamic Front." It was published three months later in the London newspaper "Al-Quds al-'Arabi."

"He used his family's connections and wealth to raise money for the Afghan resistance and provide the mujahedeen with logistical and humanitarian aid, and participated in several battles in the Afghan war. He inherited $250 million from his family's estimated $5 billion fortune. As the war with the Soviets drew to a close, bin Laden formed al Qaeda (Arabic for "the base"), an organization of ex-mujahedeen and other supporters, channeling fighters and funds to the Afghan resistance.

Once the Soviets pulled out of Afghanistan, bin Laden returned to Saudi Arabia to work for the family construction firm, the Bin Laden Group. He became involved in Saudi groups opposed to the reigning Saudi monarchy, the Fahd family."

In this context, if you would recall, US Administration also spent a lot of resources to help Afghan resistance to fight against Soviets.

Another point to remember here is the fact that there are numerous evidences to prove that Bush's family had close ties with Bin Laden's family and King Fahd's family for a very long time.

"From 1992 on, the U.S. alleges that bin Laden and other al Qaeda members decided that the group should set aside its differences with other Shiite Muslim terrorist organizations in order to cooperate against the perceived common enemy, the United States and its allies. U.S. authorities say the targets of these attacks included U.S. military forces in Saudi Arabia, and in Yemen, and U.S. forces stationed in the Horn of Africa, including Somalia."

"In 1996, bin Laden issued a "declaration of jihad," writing that his goal is to drive the U.S. military out of Saudi Arabia and overthrow the Saudi government."

"When it becomes apparent that it would be impossible to repel these Americans without assaulting them, even if this involved the killing of

Muslims, this is permissible under Islam," he said.
"Our job is to instigate"

I thought that Bin Laden might have some of his own grievances in respect of what is going on in the Middle East between Israel and Palestine. But, I couldn't find any justifiable evidence in this respect. Perhaps, he is too busy with his primary task of getting rid of American military forces from their land of the holy places. Perhaps, I haven't searched in depth.

However, the Middle East conflict is another major explosive issue and we will talk about this issue at the end of this chapter.

Okay, we know who the enemies are, and why they are practicing such terrorism.

What can we do, individually and collectively, to contain it initially and stop it eventually? I recommend a detailed study of the recent book by Richard Clarke where he traces all the evidences in this respect.

It is true that nobody should give in to the terrorists. But, at the same time, it is also true and imperative that we should study what their grievances are so that, in the interests of our National Security and safety of the citizens, we can see whether there is anything constructive we can do to alleviate this on going fear of attacks by the terrorists. I list herein, again, what seems to be the terrorists' real grievances are:

• "To fundamentalists like bin Laden, the U.S. presence is anathema because Saudi Arabia is home to "the two most holy places" in Islam -- Mecca and Medina."
• In an interview bin Laden gave to CNN in 1997, he said the ongoing U.S. military presence in Saudi Arabia is an "occupation of the land of the holy places."
•In February 1998, bin Laden issued a "fatwa," a religious ruling, calling for Muslims to kill Americans and their allies. Three other groups, including the Islamic Jihad in Egypt, endorse the ruling.
• "The ruling to kill the Americans and their allies⁻ civilians and military ⁻ is an individual duty for every Muslim who can do it in any country in which it is possible to do it, in order to liberate the al-Aqsa Mosque and

the holy mosque from their grip, and in order for their armies to move out of all the lands of Islam, defeated and unable to threaten any Muslim," the statement, issued under the "World Islamic Front" name, read. It was published three months later in the London newspaper "Al-Quds al-'Arabi."

• "In 1996, bin Laden issued a "declaration of jihad," writing that his goal is to drive the U.S. military out of Saudi Arabia and overthrow the Saudi government."

Since the end of the Gulf War, the US Military presence in Saudi Arabia became permanent. In the interest of the safety of all the American Citizens, let us think again. **If the US Military pulls out of Saudi Arabia, then there may be a chance for these terrorists to leave the Americans alone in peace leading to less or no fear of attack by these terrorists.** It is not certain. These terrorists may find some other excuse to attack American people again. Or may concentrate on the Middle East conflict and attack Israelis. We never know what they would be up to. But, if by US Military pulling out of Saudi Arabia there is going to be any chance of providing safety to American people, according to me, we must consider this option very seriously. So, as for me, **the choice for the American government is whether to stay put in Saudi Arabia to protect the interests of Bush's close family friends viz. King Fahd's family and keep a base there in line with the policy of global domination, or to pull the US Military out of Saudi Arabia hoping that this may lead to some sort of safety and security to the American people.** Personally, I will go for the second option since safety of American citizens is more important to me than protecting the interests of Bush's family friends. But, Mr. Bush, we know for certain that your aspirations of global domination and personal benefits of protecting the Fahd's family will outweigh the other sensible and safe option to protect the interests of American people.

So, it should be up to the US citizens to act in line with what they want. US citizens have to decide whether continue to blindly believe Bush's preaching and false propaganda and go though the constant fear of attacks by these terrorists, in addition to paying an exorbitant amount towards the cost to contain these terrorists' atrocities, or to persuade in every possible way they can to get the US Military out of Saudi Arabia and hope for some peace of mind. Again, it is your choice, my dear US citizens. The ball is in your court. Because the reality is, we still have a democracy, at least in theory.

So, you make it or break it, but, for heaven sake, don't just moan about it without doing the right thing at the right time.

I would like to make just one final note about Osama bin Laden' capture.

Do you remember the instance when Mr. Bush's approval rating went up just after Saddam's capture? We are so glad that Saddam has been captured and is being brought to face justice. I sincerely hope and pray that the other monster, Osama bin Laden, is also captured very soon. The search is very intense these days, maybe because of the ensuing election. I hear that he will be captured soon. I really hope so.

Please remember this. Since February 2004, suddenly, there has been a real intense search for Bin Laden. Why this type of serious and sustained search for this devil did not continue ever since September 2001? He is the one who caused, and will continue to cause, all the chaos for Americans. For any sane person, I would have thought that hunting for this evil would be the top most priority. This is what Richard Clarke is emphasizing in his recent book. But, just a minute, the Bush Administration had other top priority tasks that they couldn't afford to let go at this time, since they have been waiting for this moment for quite a while.

Please recall the following statements as per, www.abcnews.go.com/sections/nightline/DailyNews/pnac_030310.html,
"in a report just before the 2000 election that would bring Bush to power, the group predicted that the shift would come about slowly, unless there were "some catastrophic and catalyzing event, like a new Pearl Harbor."

That event came on Sept. 11, 2001. By that time, Cheney was vice president, Rumsfeld was secretary of defense, and Wolfowitz his deputy at the Pentagon.

The next morning — before it was even clear who was behind the attacks — Rumsfeld insisted at a Cabinet meeting that Saddam's Iraq should be "a principal target of the first round of terrorism," according to Bob Woodward's book Bush At War. "

That is why, instead of concentrating on capturing Osama bin Laden soon, they were seriously hell bent on going after Iraq in full swing. They can't afford to wait for another "catastrophic and catalyzing event, like a new Pearl Harbor."

But, now since January 2004, for a variety of reasons, Mr. Bush's popularity rating has been going down. So, if they capture Bin Laden now there is a real good chance of Mr. Bush's rating going up again. Because, most of the morons wouldn't know, or wouldn't want to know, the facts cited above.

But, I have a strong suspicion here about Mr. Bush's intentions, at the same time, in this context. I have a nasty feeling that the American search mission, with the help of the Pakistanis, already knows where this devil is hiding. I guess that his movements are being fully monitored and kept under strict US and Pakistani vigilance. He can be captured or the news of his capture can be released to the public at the time when the Bush Administration wants. When do you think Mr. Bush will want the people to know about this? Yes, you got that right. Not right now. If it happens now, then Mr. Bush's rating will go up momentarily and then will come down again just before the November election. Of course, they wouldn't want that to happen. So, what is the best time? My guess is that it will be sometime in late September or early October. This will give the boost Mr. Bush needs to win the election. Osama bin Laden will serve as a real good trump card. Well planned, Mr. Bush. You are a genius. You know all the dirty tricks to win the election. You have proved it beyond doubt in year 2000. First of all, as of now, you have collected so much campaign money, the likes of which nobody else in this planet earth has ever done before, since you know very well money means everything to win the election. Of course, you will accumulate more and more until the last minute. By the way, have all those rich buddies who benefited out of your massive tax cut to them returned their favor back to you by way of $2000 per seat while you go around on your campaign contribution collection? Then, of course, you can count on those people who have very little between their ears to win the election. Well done, Mr. Bush. You and your team members should be congratulated for the well-planned approach to swindle another four years of stay at 1600 Pennsylvania Avenue.

Now, let us look at what is going on in the Middle East between Israel and Palestine.

I don't want to go into the history behind this conflict between these two countries. Obviously, each side is claiming that its cause is justified. But, now that the conflict and ever increasing violence has persisted over the last so many years, the truth is that no body is telling the truth. Violence breeds violence. This is what we see as a reality in the Middle East. These two groups of people constantly fight between each other. They are not sitting at a conference table to discuss, with all sincerity, the aspects of how to get the things moving so that they may live next to each other peacefully.

In this context, I must give the due credit to Mr. Clinton, who tried his best throughout his entire period in office, including the late last moment of his Presidency, for sincerely trying to get these two parties together to iron out their differences, and to arrive at something positive for a peaceful living next to each other. Of course, the extremists on either side derailed every progress that Mr. Clinton was hoping to find.

But, what did Mr. Bush do after he moved to the White House? NOTHING. He sat on his throne for a very long time doing nothing to promote peace in that region. When serious violence erupted again he joined the Israelis' side and condemned Arafat. Is that the way to ensure peace in that region?

Suppose two of your children constantly fight against each other, what do you do as parents? Do you take side? In the interest of happy family atmosphere again, you insist and enforce that both children sit and talk to iron out their differences. This is the way you can hope to have peace at home again, if you care about both the children, but not by taking side.

America is the "super power." So, like how Mr. Carter and Mr. Clinton did, US should persuade the leaders of Israel and Palestine to get back to the conference table to iron out their differences. Give an ultimatum to both. Tell them "do it for good, or else." But, this is not happening. May be because, both democrats and republicans have become the puppets of Israeli influence. I am convinced that both the democrats and the republicans receive a considerable amount of contributions from the Israelis' special interests. As such, nothing positive that could happen is happening. Here we go again: Money talks, and money matters in everything, unfortunately.

You don't have to be a rocket scientist or a brain surgeon to understand the reasons behind the continued unrest and violence in the Middle East. My feeling is that unless, and until, the US Administration gives an ultimatum to both Israel and Palestine to iron out their differences, there is no hope of finding any peace in the Middle East. When I say ultimatum, no way I am suggesting military action in this respect. I am advocating for a peaceful boycott and isolation of both Israel and Palestine in every respect from the world community until such time they arrive at an acceptable peaceful resolution between themselves for all their issues. Unless and until the "super power" stops signaling and supporting the Israelis blindly, whether we like it or not, the terrorists attacks on American interests will continue forever. Those Palestinians are justifiably desperate even to the extent of embarking on suicide bombing. They feel that they have nothing to live for. Unfortunately, the religious fundamentalists and terrorists exploit the situation to their advantage. The whole world knows well that the Palestinians have genuine grievances. But, the American politicians blindly support the Israelis. In the interest of our own safety, and then that of the world community, let us get real and face the facts.

Mr. Bush, I have just one question and one request for you:

I just happened to read two of the best sellers (*Dude, Where's My Country* and *Stupid White Men*) by a guy called Michael Moore. He seems like a real pain in your back. He accuses you of a lot of things that I find it hard to believe. I'm sure that they are not true. For example, he accuses you of allowing the private jets to fly around the USA to pick up and evacuate the members of bin Laden family and Saudi Royal family immediately after 9/11 attacks when all other aircrafts were grounded in the USA. No, I don't believe it. You, the King and controller of the war on terror, would not have let this happen when the whole nation was in chaos searching for those foreign terrorists. Of course, you have nothing to hide. Why don't you just shut him up for good? I know that you would be busy going around the country to collect the payback payments from your rich buddies. So, ask someone in the administration to provide the facts as answers to the questions that this fellow has been on about in his books. I think he is a bit too much for anyone to handle. Only a "super power" can undertake this task. You need to do something really positive to zip his lips. But, ask your guys to be careful not to mess it up again like "AWOL" issue. Thanks.

By the way, Bush and Blair are complaining about other countries having nuclear arsenal and weapons of mass destruction. It is true we, the ordinary law abiding citizens of the world, don't want to see **ANY** country to have any of these items. But, what happened to all that massive pile up of these items in the custody of all the major Western powers, like Israel, China, India, Pakistan, etc.? Why should any of these countries possess any of these items? What justification do they have? Can any one tell me why? As for India and Pakistan, what is the matter with those guys? Millions are still starving and suffering in both the countries. What is their priority? Feeding and taking care of those poor citizens or escalating the nuclear arms race between you two? You guys need your heads tested.

Please give me one good and simple justifiable reason as to why any of these countries should have any of these items? Preaching is for others only. Is it? Before you tell others to clean up their act, you must clean up your act first. Simply because you, the Western powers and Israel, happen to be the real big bullies, you think that you guys are entitled to pile up anything you want? No questions will be asked. You are accusing Iraq, saying that Saddam is a bad guy, and he will use them against his neighbors. So, you argue that he should not have any of those items. It is true. Fair enough.

Mr. Bush, at the same time, in what way are you any better than Hitler or Mussolini or Saddam in this context? What happened to Israel's nuclear program? We never ever heard in the media about you, or for that matter, any American politician making any mention about it. How come? Israel has been occupying Palestine for years and years. You and all the American politicians blindly continue to support Israel whereas the rest of the world opposes their occupation. You invaded Iraq for oil and global domination. Tell me, in what way are you, or Ariel Sharon, any better than Saddam? Let me tell you why you two guys think that you are the God Almighty. Your attitude is simply this: "I have the best military strength anyone would like to have. So, I can do what I like, when I like and how I like. You dare to stop me. Who cares about what the UN or the rest of the world thinks of us?" This is your attitude and you two guys have no regard or respect for the rest of human beings purely because you are big bullies and just arrogant. This is a proven and well-demonstrated fact.

If only **EVERY** country on this planet earth happened to be free from any of these weapons, how nice and safe this planet would turn out to be? Can you imagine this hypothetical scenario just for a moment? Just think about it. Having said that, in the interest of everybody on this planet earth, let us just consider the following purely hypothetical scenario. I know very well that it would never, ever happen here, or anywhere in the world. But, there is no harm in just dreaming and wishing for real good things to happen to everyone. Is there?

The US citizens carefully select and elect real good members for their governments, in particular the Federal Government. So, the governments now have people's representatives who are really dedicated to serve their people. Don't laugh. I told you already that it would never ever happen in the USA. May be in other countries, but definitely not in the USA. I am just dreaming. The President takes the lead to persuade the entire world to the effect that every country should effective immediate

- Stop producing, buying and selling any type of weapons of mass destruction, chemical and biological weapons,
- Destroy every one of these items that they already have,
- Arrange for verifiable inspection to ensure that none of these items ever exist any more anywhere in the world, and
- Use the talents of all those intellectuals who were engaged in designing and manufacturing these weapons of mass destruction to work towards ensuring better environmental condition, better health care, finding cure for various diseases like cancer, HIV, etc.

How nice it would be, if only it could happen. I said that it is just my dream.

If you would please recall, I emphasized before that American citizens have more responsibility than the citizens of the rest of the world. Even though it is just my dream, you guys can make it an American dream, if you want to. You have the power to make it happen. Like what happened in the United Kingdom before, you can ensure landslide victory for those who really care about the hard working, middle, and low-income groups of people.

Please checkout the past records of both the democrats and republicans. Don't forget the republicans' record, in particular. These republicans wasted so much of taxpayer's money and valuable working hours in the congress in their attempt to derail Mr. Clinton when he was in the White House. According to me, these guys should never ever be elected to any office. But, unfortunately, I know that it won't happen purely because most of the "middle of the road" category of people in the USA doesn't really understand the power they have, nor do they use that power for the good of this great nation. What can I say? Just whine and moan, as usual. That is all I can do. You can take a horse to the water, but you cannot make it drink. The horse should want to drink. Exactly same situation is here now. You, each and every one of you, must want to bring a sane and sensible government. There is no point in others talking about it.

I list below just two more items for you to think about.

Please checkout this site for a real shocking revelation regarding the dangers of flying. As per the website, *http://www.wishtv.com/global/ story.asp?s=1897865&ClientType=Printable,*

"Nearly three years after September 11th, air cargo security remains largely unchanged at Indianapolis International Airport and airports across the country. Half the belly of every passenger plane is filled with unscreened cargo. Congress's most vocal critic finds this unacceptable. He lays the blame on the shoulders of the Transportation Security Administration."
Please check out the following site for a real shocking revelation regarding the dangers of the massive pile up of weapons of mass destruction that we have in the USA. Shouldn't we get rid of each and every one of those weapons of mass destruction in the interest of the safety of our citizens? Shouldn't this be our top most priority to protect our citizens? You decide. It is your life and your country we are talking about. Unless you become a pain in the back, and pester the politicians to get rid of these types of weapons for good from your own homeland first, and then everywhere else in the world, there is no real hope for any safe living within the USA.
The following is an extract from the website, *http://www.wishtv.com/global/ story.asp?s=1827540&ClientType=Printable,*

"The danger of terror and weapons of mass destruction comes home to Indiana. Even the US Army says, 'The continued storage of these stockpiles represents a significant threat. Destroying (it)...will eliminate a significant terrorist target for our nation.' - (Colonel Jesse Barber)."
"'Clearly as long as VX is in Indiana, the danger of exposure to deadly

gasses is there,' said Senator Richard Lugar (R-IN)."

"'If one of those 9/11 aircraft landed in Newport at the stockpile, it would be the worst catastrophe potentially in the history of the world,' said Paul Walker, Global Green."

"Tornadoes Also Pose Threat. Terrorists are not the only concern. For years, Indiana officials have worried about tornadoes making the VX nerve agent airborne."

"'Those canisters are not very heavy - only about 3,200 pounds, which is the size of a small car and in this last outbreak of tornadoes, we saw cars flung all over the place,' said Jerry Hauer, former Indiana State Emergency Management Agency Director.

Hauer, who is now a Washington-based terrorism expert, has warned about Newport for more than a decade. Fourteen years ago he watched as a tornado passed within one mile of the deadly VX stockpile.

'It's only a matter of time before the odds catch up with you and something blows through that facility,' he said, 'And you'd have VX all over the place.'"

"Indiana's storage site of the deadly VX nerve agent is not only vulnerable from the air, ground and weather. There is also the threat of earthquakes. Indiana sits on the New Madrid fault line. Experts say Hoosiers could feel the shocks from Newport to Indianapolis."

"A Deadly Accident
Remember: the concern is making the VX, a substance like motor oil, airborne and aerosolized. It happened in Utah. During testing, just twenty pounds of VX was accidentally released to the wind. More than 6,000 sheep were killed up to forty miles away.
If it happened here, it would cut a deadly path nearly to Danville. Only twenty pounds of the VX killed over 6,000 sheep. Indiana stores 1,200 tons.
Sen. Lugar, Indiana's senior senator, has been successful getting rid of weapons of mass destruction in Washington. But he agrees it is still a challenge to protect Hoosiers from the deadly VX sitting in Indiana."
"'The intersection of terrorism and weapons of mass destruction is the ultimate

event that could change the course of our history,' said Sen. Lugar. It could also change how the US approaches security."

"Security Concerns

The deadliest chemical weapon in the world sits in Indiana, separated from the outside only by a simple chain link fence topped with barbed wire. No one, no armed guard, ever stopped us. No one ever questioned us. Some may wonder why we are reporting this. Authorities tell us terrorists and enemies of the United States already know most of this. They are well aware of our vulnerabilities. The point of our investigation is to focus on improving our defenses and strengthening homeland security in Indiana."

Points for *Something to Think About*:

- We should be ever so grateful to the brave men and women (military personnel, National Guards, Reservists, Fire Fighters and law enforcing personnel) who work so hard and sacrifice their own lives for our safe living. Let us pray to our God to bless them all.
- What is more important than our right to live in our own community free from the fear of robbery, rape, vandalism, murder, gang violence, drive by shooting, etc.? We must insist that the law makers and government officials get this issue as one of their top most priorities item to successfully resolve very soon.

- Life is short. We don't know what is in store for us the next minute.
- Out of all those brave men and women in Iraq, already killed or seriously wounded or who are still out there risking their lives every minute, how many happen to be the close family members and friends of those warmongers? Next to Nothing.
- The West, in particular the USA, created and nurtured Saddam in 1980s to keep Iran under control. The US policy then was to export all types of products from the US, including weapons of mass destruction, to both Iraq and Iran to fight against each other.
- It is proved beyond doubt that Saddam Hussein did NOT pose any imminent threat to the USA prior to the recent Iraq invasion.

• Iraq invasion was well planned by Bush Administration even before September 11 attack.

• Iraq invasion is a part of the big plan of the Bush Administration, viz. American global domination and the control of oil in the Middle East for American advantage.

• The rest of the world population rallied behind America during the Gulf War and to eradicate the followers of Bin Laden. But, they do not support the present Iraq invasion because it is unjustified in every sense of the word.

• The rest of the world is better informed of what is going on with American politics since the foreign media, unlike the American media, has no fear of any type of reprisal from the right wing American Administration.

• The real beneficiaries of the Iraq invasion and occupation are the big corporations like Halliburton who have been generous with their contributions to the Republicans. We, the taxpayers, are the losers since we are paying for everything related to this war.

Please checkout *http://www.brillig.com/debt_clock/* for everything related to the national debt. The ever-increasing national debt is to be paid back by the present and future taxpayers. They have to work ever so hard to pay back this debt that Mr. Bush is creating.

• Iraq invasion was for oil and for American global domination at the expense of so many lives in Iraq and enormous national debt in the US.

• Mujahedeen received every possible support and help from both the US Administration and Osama Bin Laden for their fight against the Russians.

• Bin Laden's goal is to drive the U.S. military out of Saudi Arabia and overthrow the Saudi government. If by pulling the US military out of Saudi Arabia, the land of their holy places, American people can hope to have some peace of mind free from the fear of attacks by these terrorists, then this option should be considered seriously for immediate action. American people should force the politicians to do so. Our safety is more important than American global domination and protecting Bush's family friends in Saudi Arabia.

• It is a strong possibility that Bin Laden's capture will be announced to the world sometime just before the November 2004 election as a boost for Mr. Bush to win the election.

• Unless and until US Administration gives ultimatum to both Israel and Palestine to iron out their differences peacefully at conference table, there is no hope of finding any peace in the Middle East. The ultimatum should be to the effect "do it for good or else."

• Before you tell others to clean up their act, you must clean up your act first.

• In what way Mr. Bush or Ariel Sharon is any better than Hitler or Mussolini or Saddam?

• America and Israel have no regard or respect for the views of the rest of the world purely because they have mighty military strength.

• If only **EVERY** country in this planet happens to be free from any of the weapons of mass destruction, how nice and safe this planet would turn out to be?

Did Bush Press For Iraq-9/11 Link?
March 21, 2004

In the aftermath of Sept. 11, President Bush ordered his then top anti-terrorism adviser to look for a link between Iraq and the attacks, despite being told there didn't seem to be one.

The charge comes from the advisor, Richard Clarke, in an exclusive interview on *60 Minutes*.

Clarke helped shape U.S. policy on terrorism under President Reagan and the first President Bush. He was held over by President Clinton to be his terrorism czar, then held over again by the current President Bush.

In the *60 Minutes* interview and the book, Clarke tells what happened behind the scenes at the White House before, during and after Sept. 11.

"Frankly," he said, "I find it outrageous that the president is running for re-election on the grounds that he's done such great things about terrorism. He ignored it. He ignored terrorism for months, when maybe we could have done something to stop 9/11. Maybe. We'll never know."

Clarke went on to say, "I think he's done a terrible job on the war against terrorism."

Clarke says that as early as the day after the attacks, Secretary of Defense Donald Rumsfeld was pushing for retaliatory strikes on Iraq, even though al Qaeda was based in Afghanistan.

As Clarke writes in his book, he expected the administration to focus its military response on Osama bin Laden and al Qaeda. He says he was surprised that the talk quickly turned to Iraq.

"Rumsfeld was saying that we needed to bomb Iraq," Clarke said to Stahl. "And we all said ... no, no. Al-Qaeda is in Afghanistan. We need to bomb Afghanistan. And Rumsfeld said there aren't any good targets in Afghanistan. And there are lots of good targets in Iraq. I said, 'Well, there are lots of good targets in lots of places, but Iraq had nothing to do with it.'"

"I think they wanted to believe that there was a connection, but the CIA was sitting there, the FBI was sitting there, I was sitting there saying, we've looked at this issue for years. For years we've looked and there's just no connection."

Clarke says he and CIA Director George Tenet told that to Rumsfeld, Secretary of State Colin Powell, and Attorney General John Ashcroft.

Clarke then tells Stahl of being pressured by Mr. Bush.

"The president dragged me into a room with a couple of other people, shut the door, and said, 'I want you to find whether Iraq did this.' Now he never said, 'Make it up.' But the entire conversation left me in absolutely no doubt that George Bush wanted me to come back with a report that said Iraq did this.

"I said, 'Mr. President. We've done this before. We have been looking at this. We looked at it with an open mind. There's no connection.'

"He came back at me and said, "Iraq! Saddam! Find out if there's a connection.' And in a very intimidating way. I mean that we should come back with that answer. We wrote a report."
Clarke continued, "It was a serious look. We got together all the FBI

experts, all the CIA experts. We wrote the report. We sent the report out to CIA and found FBI and said, 'Will you sign this report?' They all cleared the report. And we sent it up to the president and it got bounced by the National Security Advisor or Deputy. It got bounced and sent back saying, 'Wrong answer. ... Do it again.'

"I have no idea, to this day, if the president saw it, because after we did it again, it came to the same conclusion. And frankly, I don't think the people around the president show him memos like that. I don't think he sees memos that he doesn't-- wouldn't like the answer."

Clarke was the president's chief adviser on terrorism, yet it wasn't until Sept. 11 that he ever got to brief Mr. Bush on the subject. Clarke says that prior to Sept. 11, the administration didn't take the threat seriously.

"We had a terrorist organization that was going after us! Al Qaeda. That should have been the first item on the agenda. And it was pushed back and back and back for months.

"There's a lot of blame to go around, and I probably deserve some blame, too. But on January 24th, 2001, I wrote a memo to Condoleezza Rice asking for, urgently -- underlined urgently -- a Cabinet-level meeting to deal with the impending al Qaeda attack. And that urgent memo-- wasn't acted on.

"I blame the entire Bush leadership for continuing to work on Cold War issues when they were brought back in power in 2001. It was as though they were preserved in amber from when they left office eight years earlier. They came back. They wanted to work on the same issues right away: Iraq, Star Wars. Not new issues, the new threats that had developed over the preceding eight years."

Clarke finally got his meeting about al Qaeda in April, three months after his urgent request. But it wasn't with the president or cabinet. It was with the second-in-command in each relevant department.

For the Pentagon, it was Paul Wolfowitz.

Clarke relates, "I began saying, 'We have to deal with bin Laden; we have to deal with al Qaeda.' Paul Wolfowitz, the Deputy Secretary of Defence, said, 'No, no, no. We don't have to deal with al Qaeda. Why are we talking about that little guy? We have to talk about Iraqi terrorism against the United States.'"

"And I said, 'Paul, there hasn't been any Iraqi terrorism against the United States in eight years!' And I turned to the deputy director of the CIA and said, 'Isn't that right?' And he said, 'Yeah, that's right. There is no Iraqi terrorism against the United States.'"

Clarke went on to add, "There's absolutely no evidence that Iraq was supporting al Qaeda, ever."

By June 2001, there still hadn't been a Cabinet-level meeting on terrorism, even though U.S. intelligence was picking up an unprecedented level of ominous chatter.

The CIA director warned the White House, Clarke points out. "George Tenet was saying to the White House, saying to the president - because he briefed him every morning - a major al Qaeda attack is going to happen against the United States somewhere in the world in the weeks and months ahead. He said that in June, July, and August.

Clarke says the last time the CIA had picked up a similar level of chatter was in December 1999, when Clarke was the terrorism czar in the Clinton White House.

Clarke says Mr. Clinton ordered his Cabinet to go to battle stations— meaning, they went on high alert, holding meetings nearly every day.

That, Clarke says, helped thwart a major attack on Los Angeles International Airport, when an al Qaeda operative was stopped at the border with Canada, driving a car full of explosives.

Clarke harshly criticizes President Bush for not going to battle stations when the CIA warned him of a comparable threat in the months before Sept. 11: "He never thought it was important enough for him to hold a meeting on the subject, or for him to order his National Security Adviser to hold a Cabinet-level meeting on the subject."

Finally, says Clarke, "The cabinet meeting I asked for right after the inauguration took place-- one week prior to 9/11."

In that meeting, Clarke proposed a plan to bomb al Qaeda's sanctuary in Afghanistan, and to kill bin Laden.

"The president heard those warnings. The president met daily with ... George Tenet and his staff. They kept him fully informed and at one point the president became somewhat impatient with us and said, 'I'm tired of swatting flies. Where's my new strategy to eliminate al Qaeda?'"

PNAC Seeks Global Domination
by Shirley Howland,
BulletinBoardForPeace.org, Jan. 01-04; Observer, Nov. 28-03

A blueprint for US global domination, the Project for the new American Century or PNAC, reveals that Bush and his backers were planning a premeditated attack on Iraq to secure "regime change" long before Bush took power in January 2001.

The plan shows Bush's cabinet intended to take military control of the Gulf region whether or not Saddam Hussein was in power. It says: The United States has for decades sought to play a more permanent role in Gulf regional "security." The conflict with Iraq provided the immediate justification, the need for a substantial American force presence in the Gulf. On 9/12/01, at a meeting of the National Security Council, Rumsfeld said, "We should use this opportunity to go after Iraq." And the opportunity was also seized to ram through Congress the 300 page plus Patriot Act before anyone had a chance to read it.

The PNAC declares that the "American grand strategy" must be advanced for "as far into the future as possible." It also calls for the US to "fight and decisively win multiple, simultaneous major theatre wars" as a "core mission."

The PNAC blueprint supports an earlier document written by Wolfowitz and Libby that said the US must "discourage advanced industrial nations from challenging our leadership or even aspiring to a larger regional or global role."

The PNAC report also:

- refers to key allies such as the UK as "the most effective and efficient means of exercising American global leadership;"
- describes peace-keeping missions as "demanding American political leadership rather than that of the United Nations;"
- reveals worries in the administration that Europe could rival the USA;
- says "even should Saddam pass from the scene" bases in Saudi Arabia and Kuwait will remain permanently -- despite domestic opposition in the Gulf regimes to the stationing of US troops -- as "Iran may well prove as large a threat to US interests as Iraq has;"
- spotlights China for "regime change" saying "it is time to increase the presence of American forces in southeast Asia." This, it says, may lead to American and allied power providing the spur to the process of democratisation in China;"
- calls for the creation of "US Space Forces," to dominate space, and the total control of cyberspace to prevent "enemies" using the internet against the US;
- hints that, despite threatening war against Iraq for developing weapons of mass destruction, the US may consider developing biological weapons —which the nation has banned—in decades to come. It says: "New methods of attack—electronic, "non-lethal," biological—will be more widely available ... combat likely will take place in new dimensions, in space, cyberspace, and perhaps the world of microbes ... advanced forms of biological warfare that can "target" specific genotypes may transform biological warfare from the realm of terror to a politically useful tool;"
- and pinpoints North Korea, Libya, Syria and Iran as dangerous regimes and says their existence justifies the creation of a "world-wide command-and-control system."

Tam Dalyell, the Labour MP, father of the House of Commons and one of the leading rebel voices against war with Iraq, said: "This is garbage from right-wing think-tanks stuffed with chicken-hawks—men who have never seen the horror of war, but are in love with the idea of war. Men like Cheney, who were draft-dodgers in the Vietnam war.

"This is a blueprint for US world domination—a new world order of their making. These are the thought processes of fantasist Americans who want to control the world. I am appalled that a British Labour Prime Minister should have got into bed with a crew which has this moral standing."

The Plan, or Pax Americana aka the American Empire, refers to the Project for the New American Century. The Report explains why you will not hear anyone in Washington naming a date that the Troops will be coming home. In fact, the President has repeatedly said the occupation of Iraq is going to take years...

Americans have to decide whether or not they want to rule the world, at a price of trillions of dollars, and countless lives; whether or not they want the nuclear holocaust that is bound to follow this government's attempt at Empire! The military and financial objectives of the PNAC are well on their way to being met as most Americans stand silently by, wave their flags, and pay their taxes.

———————————————

The following is the contents of
http://www.alternet.org/story.html?StoryID=16784

US Plan for Global Domination Tops Project Censored's Annual List
By *Kari Lydersen*, AlterNet
September 17, 2003

We know a lot more now about the dangers and disasters of U.S. empire building in Iraq – the ongoing bloodshed on the ground, expansion of terrorist activities, the huge budget busting costs of occupation, the stretching and undermining of the military, and the increased sense of fear and insecurity that many Americans feel as a result of the invasion and its potential for blowback.

We also now have a better handle on the immediate and flimsy reasons for the invasion. Bush told us we were going to war in Iraq because Saddam Hussein had weapons of mass destruction that threatened us; he was reconstituting his nuclear weapons programs (the aluminum tubes, the uranium from Africa); he had huge stocks of chemical and biological weapons that could be launched somehow in a way that threatened the US. And finally that Saddam was working with Al Qaeda. According to some polls, as much as 70 percent of the public believed this. But now it seems clear these were all falsehoods. The lies and deceptions Bush and his minions were feeding to the media are making their way into public discourse and are being covered fairly extensively in the press, in columns by Paul Krugman and Maureen Dowd in the NY Times and in wide ranging reporting at the Washington Post, and elsewhere.

But far, far less is known about the planning and the actors that brought us this foreign policy disaster? What ideas and world views motivated the push to overreach and try to dominate the globe, with Iraq as step number one? What secrets, maneuvers behind the scenes, and policy power struggles, after the attacks of 9/11, led the U.S. to invade a country that had nothing to do with 9/11?

The reminder that the media often reports the "news" as fed to it by those in power, and skips past the real news – the reasons for the behaviors and policies – is good reason for the continued existence of Project Censored, a program in its 27th year, that collects under-reported stories from around the country and compiles a list of the top 10 "censored stories" as well as 15 runner-ups. About 200 students and faculty from Sonoma State University compiled and reviewed the stories for Project Censored. The project describes its mission "to stimulate responsible journalists to provide more mass media coverage of those under-covered issues, and to encourage the general public to demand mass media coverage of those issues or to seek information from other sources."

Most of the stories on Project Censored's Top Ten relate to the US's war on terrorism and the invasion of Iraq. On the one hand, this emphasis indicates how the issue dominates the news, but on the other, how news consumers really understand very little about how it happened and why. Taken together, these stories paint a chilling picture of a long-ranging plan to dominate huge sections of the globe militarily and economically, and to silence dissent, curb civil liberties and undermine workers' rights in the course of it. Some of the information published as part of the project is pretty shocking, like the fact that the US removed 8,000 incriminating pages from Iraq's weapons report to the UN; or that Donald Rumsfeld may have a plan to deliberately provoke terrorists so we can react. Other issues like the attacks on civil liberties have been covered in the mainstream press, but not in the comprehensive way Project Censored would like to see.

The "Top Ten Censored Stories" followed by the 15 runner-ups:

1. The Neoconservative Plan for Global Dominance

Sources: The Sunday Herald (9/15/02), Harper's Magazine (10/02), Mother Jones (3/03), Pilger.com (12/12/02)

Project Censored has decided that the incredible lack of public knowledge of the US plan for total global domination, represented by the Project for a New American Century (PNAC) represents the media's biggest failure over the past year. The PNAC plans advocated the attacks on Iraq and Afghanistan and other current foreign policy objectives, long before the Sept. 11 terrorist attacks.

Chillingly, one document published by the PNAC in 2000 actually describes *the need for a "new Pearl Harbor"* to persuade the American public to accept the acts of war and aggression the administration wants to carry out. "But most people in the country are totally unaware that the PNAC exists," said Peter Phillips, a professor at Sonoma State and major domo of The Project Censored Project, "and that failure has aided and abetted this disaster in Iraq."

According to Project Censored authors. "In the 1970s, the United States and the Middle East were embroiled in a tug-of-war over oil. At the time, the prospect of seizing control of Arab oil fields by force was considered out of line. Still, the idea of Middle East dominance was very attractive to a group of hard-line Washington insiders that included Dick Cheney, Donald Rumsfeld, Paul Wolfowitz, Richard Perle, William Kristol and other operatives. During the Clinton years they were active in conservative think tanks like the PNAC. When Bush was elected they came roaring back into power.

In an update for the Project Censored Web site, Mother Jones writer Robert Dreyfuss notes "There was very little examination in the media of the role of oil in American policy towards Iraq and the Persian Gulf, and what coverage did exist tended to pooh-pooh or debunk the idea that the war had anything to do with it."

2. Homeland Security Threatens Civil Liberties

Sources: Global Outlook (Winter 2003), Rense.com (2-11-03 & Global Outlook, Volume 4), Center for Public Integrity (publicintegrity.org) Corporate Media partial coverage: Atlanta Journal-constitution (5/11/03/), The Tampa Tribune (3/28/03), Baltimore Sun (2/21/03)

While the media did cover the Patriot Act, and the so-called Patriot Act II, which was leaked to the press in February 2003, there wasn't sufficient analysis of some of the truly dangerous and precedent-setting components of both acts. This goes especially for the shocking provision in Patriot II that would allow even US citizens to be treated as enemy combatants and held without counsel, simply on suspicion of connections to terrorism.

"Under section 501 a US citizen engaging in lawful activity can be picked off the streets, or from home, and taken to a secret military tribunal with no access to, or notification of, a lawyer, the press, or family." This would be considered justified if the agent "inferred from the conduct" suspicious intention.

Fortunately Patriot I is under major duress in Congress as both parties are supporting significant revisions. Yet, President Bush, realizing that he and his unpopular Attorney General John Ashcroft are losing popular support, is threatening a veto, and has aggressively gone on the offense in favor of the repugnant Patriot II. Let's see if the media has learned its lesson from Patriot I. Will it probe the new legislation much more thoroughly than the first round, which received inadequate analysis post 9/11?

3. US Illegally Removes Pages from Iraq UN Report

Source: The Humanist and ArtVoice (March/April 2003), first covered by
Amy Goodman on Democracy Now!

Story three is the shockingly under-reported fact that the Bush
administration removed a whopping 8,000 of 11,800 pages from the report
the Iraqi government submitted to the UN Security Council and the
International Atomic Energy Agency. The pages included details on how the
US had actually supplied Iraq with chemical and biological weapons and the
building blocks for weapons of mass destruction. The pages reportedly
implicate not only Reagan and Bush administration officials, but also major
corporations including Bechtel, Eastman Kodak and Dupont, and the US
Departments of Energy and Agriculture.

In comments to Project Censored, Michael Niman, author of one of the
articles cited, noted that his article was based on secondary sources, mostly
from the international press, since the topic received an almost complete
blackout in the US press. Referring to his first Project Censored nomination
in 1989, in which he went into the bush in Costa Rica, he said, "With such
thorough self-censorship in the US press, reading the international press is
now akin to going into the remote bush."

4. Rumsfeld's Plan to Provoke Terrorists
Source: CounterPunch (11/1/02)

Moscow Times columnist and CounterPunch contributor Chris Floyd
developed this story off a small item in the LA Times in October 2002 about
secret armies the Pentagon has been developing around the world. "The Pro-
active, Preemptive Operations Group (or "Pee-Twos") will carry out secret
missions designed to 'stimulate reactions' among terrorist groups, provoking
them into committing violent acts which would then expose them to
'counterattack' by US forces," Floyd wrote. "The Pee-Twos will thus come
in handy whenever the Regime hankers to add a little oil-laden real estate or
a new military base to the Empire's burgeoning portfolio. Just find a nest of
violent malcontents, stir 'em with a stick, and presto: instant justification for

whatever level of intervention-conquest-raping that you might desire."

Floyd notes that while the story received considerable play in international and alternative media, it has hardly been mentioned in the mainstream US press.

"At first glance, this decided lack of interest might seem a curious reaction, given the American media's insatiable – and profitable – obsession with terrorism," he told Project Censored. "But the media's equally intense abhorrence of moral ambiguity – especially when it involves possible American complicity in mayhem and murder – makes the silence easier to understand."

5. The Effort to Make Unions Disappear

Sources: Z Magazine, (11/20/02), War Times (10/11 2002), The Progressive (11/03), The American Prospect (3/03)

The war on terrorism has also had the convenient side benefit for conservatives of making it easier for employers and the government to suppress organized labor in the name of national security. For example, in October 2002 Bush was able to force striking International Longshore and Warehouse Union members back to work in the San Francisco Bay Area in the name of national safety.

Chicago journalist Lee Sustar noted that labor coverage is usually woefully inadequate in the mainstream media, even though union membership, while shrinking, still makes up a national constituency 13 million strong.

"Twenty years ago every paper had a beat reporter on labor who knew what was going on," he said. "Today that's not the case. Besides a token story on Labor Day or a human-interest story here and there, you don't see coverage of labor. You only see coverage from the business side." said Sustar, Although Steven Greenhouse, the labor reporter for the New York Times is one obvious exception to Sustar's claim.

Ann Marie Cusac, whose story for The Progressive about the decimation of unions was cited, said she thinks the position of organized labor is worse than it has ever been.

She combed National Labor Relations Board files for egregious examples of the lengths to which employers will go to bust unions. And she found a lot. "They had a woman with carpal tunnel syndrome pulling nails out of boards above her head, because they wanted her to go on disability so she couldn't organize," she said. "But she did it, even knowing she might disable herself. The willingness of people to sacrifice, because they know how important it is to unionize, is a sign of hope."

6. Closing Access to Information Technology

Source: Dollars and Sense (9/02)

The potential closing of access to digital information is a development that could have a harmful effect on the powerful role online media plays in side stepping media gate keepers and keeping people better informed. "The FCC and Congress are currently overturning the public-interest rules that have encouraged the expansion of the Internet up until now," writes Arthur Stamoulis, whose story was published in Dollars and Sense.

The Internet currently provides a buffet of independent and international media sources to counter the mostly homogenous offerings of mainstream US media, especially broadcast.

As the shift to broadband gains momentum, cable companies are trying hard to dominate the market, and eventually control access.

In 2002 the Federal Communications Commission (FCC) decided to allow cable networks to avoid common carrier requirements. Now the giant phone companies, who offer the competitive DSL services, want the same freedoms to control access to their lines. In the long run, instead of the thousands of small ISP services to choose from, the switch from dial-up to broadband means that users will have less and less choice over who provides their internet access.

While the media finally woke up and gave significant coverage to the recent public rebellion against the FCC, which voted to increase media concentration even further, there has been scant coverage to the problem that the Internet as we know it might be lost.

7. Treaty Busting By the United States

Sources: Connections (6/02), The Nation (4/02), Ashville Global Report (6/20-26/02), Global Outlook (Summer 2002)

"The US is a signatory to nine multilateral treaties that it has either blatantly violated or gradually subverted," says Project Censored. These include the Comprehensive Test Ban Treaty, the Treaty Banning Antipersonnel Mines and the Kyoto Protocol on global warming. Just as the Bush administration is crowing about the possibility of Saddam Hussein manufacturing nuclear or chemical weapons, it is violating treaties meant to curb these threats, including the nuclear Non-Proliferation Treaty and the Chemical Weapons Commission.

8. US/British Forces Continue Use of Depleted Uranium Weapons Despite Massive Evidence of Negative Health Effects

Sources: The Sunday Herald (3/30/03), Hustler Magazine (6/03), Children of War (3/03)

The eighth story on the list deals with another subject that victims have tried to get into the mainstream media for over a decade – the US's use of depleted uranium in Iraq, in both the recent invasion and in the Gulf War. Depleted uranium (DU) was also used in Afghanistan, Kosovo and Bosnia.

The writers cited, including the hard-core porn magazine Hustler, note that cancer rates have skyrocketed in Iraq since the first Gulf War, most likely because of the massive contamination of the soil with DU from the explosive, armor-piercing munitions. US soldiers are also victims of this travesty, suffering Gulf War syndrome, and other ailments, that many feel sure are linked to their exposure to DU.

Reese Erlich, a freelance journalist who reported on the topic for a syndicated radio broadcast and related web site report, said that the federal government has dealt with the issue of DU the way the tobacco industry deals with its liability problems. "They'll fog the issue so no one can say for sure what's happening," he said. "They'll commission studies so they can say, 'There are conflicting reports,' 'We need more information.'"

He noted that while the US media is quiet about the issue, it is a hot topic in the international press. "When you get outside the US, the media is much more critical," he said. "They refer to it as a weapon of mass destruction. This will be a legacy the US has left in Iraq. Long after the electricity is repaired and the oil wells are pumping, children will be getting cancer. The US knew this would happen, it can't claim ignorance."

9. In Afghanistan: Poverty, Women's Rights and Civil Disruption Worse then Ever

Sources: The Nation (10/14/02), Left Turn (3-4/03), The Nation (4/29/02), Mother Jones (7-8/02) Mainstream Coverage: Toronto Star (3/2/03)

Though his work isn't cited here, Erlich also reported on the topic of the ninth story on the list, the continuing poverty, civil disruption and repression of women in Afghanistan. While the country has virtually dropped off the radar screen in the US press and public consciousness, it is suffering its worst decade of poverty ever. Warlords and tribal fiefdoms continue to rule the country, and women are as repressed as ever, contrary to the feel-good images of burqa-stripping that have been broadcast in the media here.

"Reporters by and large don't go to Afghanistan to report on what they see," said Erlich, who spent several weeks reporting in the country. "They go to the state department officials, so everything is filtered through these rose-colored glasses, saying things are getting better. But they're not."

10. Africa Faces New Threat of New Colonialism

Source: Left Turn (7-8/02), Briarpatch, Vol. 32, No. 1, Excerpted from The CCPA Monitor, (10/02), New Internationalist (1-2/03)

While Afghanistan is being essentially ignored, the tenth story on the list shows how African countries are getting plenty of attention from the US – but not the kind of attention they need. These stories deal with the formation in June, 2002 of the New Partnership for Africa's Development, or NEPAD, by a group of leaders from the world's eight most powerful countries (the G8) who claim to be carrying out an anti-poverty campaign for the continent. But the group doesn't include the head of a single African nation, and critics charge that the plan is more about opening the continent to international investment and looting its resources than fighting poverty.

"NEPAD is akin to Plan Colombia in its attempt to employ Western development techniques to provide economic opportunities for international investment," says Project Censored.

The Project Censored awards ceremony will take place Oct. 4 in San Rafael, Calif. For tickets or more information, visit the Web site at www.projectcensored.org.

The 15 stories cited as runners-up to the top ten most censored stories of the year are the following:

#11: U.S. Implicated in Taliban Massacre
#12: Bush Administration Behind Failed Military Coup in Venezuela
#13: Corporate Personhood Challenged
#14: Unwanted Refugees a Global Problem
#15: U.S. Military's War on the Earth
#16: Plan Puebla-Panama and the FTAA
#17: Clear Channel Monopoly Draws Criticism
#18: Charter Forest Proposal Threatens Access to Public Lands
#19: U.S. Dollar vs. the Euro: Another Reason for the Invasion of Iraq
#20: Pentagon Increases Private Military Contracts
#21: Third World Austerity Policies: Coming Soon to a City Near You
#22: Welfare Reform Up For Reauthorization, but Still No Safety Net
#23: Argentina Crisis Sparks Cooperative Growth
#24: Aid to Israel Fuels Repressive Occupation in Palestine
#25: Convicted Corporations Receive Perks Instead of Punishment

An Elusive Enemy

The U.S. presence in Saudi Arabia fuels Osama bin Laden's jihad

Posted January 2001

(CNN) -- In winning the Persian Gulf War, the United States also made itself a resourceful and elusive enemy in the form of accused terrorist mastermind Osama bin Laden.

The son of a Saudi Arabian businessman, bin Laden has called for a Muslim jihad, or holy war, against the United States. He has encouraged Muslims to kill all the Americans—civilian or military—they can.

His rage stems from the decision by Saudi Arabia to allow the United States to use the country as a staging area for attacks on Iraqi forces in Kuwait and Iraq. After the victory, the U.S. military presence became permanent.

To fundamentalists like bin Laden, the U.S. presence is anathema because Saudi Arabia is home to "the two most holy places" in Islam—Mecca and Medina. Mecca is the birthplace of Mohammed and the location of the Great Mosque of Mecca, considered by Muslims to be the most sacred spot on Earth. Mecca also is the destination of the hajj, the pilgrimage that is one of five tenets of Islam. All Muslims who are physically and financially able are expected to perform the hajj at least once.

One of the rituals of the hajj is to circle the Kaaba, a black-draped, oblong stone building located inside the mosque. The Koran says the Kaaba is the oldest house of worship in the world, and during the hajj, pilgrims circle it seven times. It is toward the Kaaba—believed to rest on the spot where, in the Bible, Abraham was prepared to sacrifice his son Isaac before God stayed his hand and substituted a ram—that Muslims face to pray.

In an interview bin Laden gave to CNN in 1997, he said the ongoing U.S. military presence in Saudi Arabia is an "occupation of the land of the holy places."

In February 1998, bin Laden issued a "fatwa," a religious ruling, calling for Muslims to kill Americans and their allies. Three other groups, including the Islamic Jihad in Egypt, endorse the ruling.

"The ruling to kill the Americans and their allies— civilians and military —is an individual duty for every Muslim who can do it in any country in which it is possible to do it, in order to liberate the al-Aqsa Mosque and the holy mosque from their grip, and in order for their armies to move out of all the lands of Islam, defeated and unable to threaten any Muslim," the statement, issued under the "World Islamic Front" name, read. It was published three months later in the London newspaper "Al-Quds al-'Arabi."

Son of a wealthy Saudi businessman Osama bin Laden is one of 52 children sired by Muhammad bin Laden and born to one of his 10 wives. The elder bin Laden emigrated from a remote area of neighboring Yemen to Saudi Arabia as a young man and built the largest construction company in the Saudi kingdom.

The bin Laden family was recognized for its commitment to Islam and the young bin Laden met and studied with various Muslim scholars as he grew up. His writings reflect his Islamic training blended with a harsh political perspective.

In 1979, after the Soviet invasion of Afghanistan, a 22-year-old bin Laden traveled there to fight the Soviets alongside the Afghan resistance fighters known as the mujahedeen.

He used his family's connections and wealth to raise money for the Afghan resistance and provide the mujahedeen with logistical and humanitarian aid, and participated in several battles in the Afghan war. He inherited $250 million from his family's estimated $5 billion fortune.

As the war with the Soviets drew to a close, bin Laden formed al Qaeda (Arabic for "the base"), an organization of ex-mujahedeen and other supporters channeling fighters and funds to the Afghan resistance.

Once the Soviets pulled out of Afghanistan, bin Laden returned to Saudi Arabia to work for the family construction firm, the Bin Laden Group. He became involved in Saudi groups opposed to the reigning Saudi monarchy, the Fahd family.

Opposition views cause him to flee Saudi Arabia

He opposed the Saudi decision to allow the U.S. military into the country after the Iraqi invasion of Kuwait and fled Saudi Arabia in 1991 after he was confined to the port city of Jeddah for his opposition to the Saudi-U.S. alliance.

Since then, bin Laden has lived in Afghanistan and the Sudan, where a Muslim government gained control in 1989 after a coup. Its new government adopted a policy allowing any Muslim into the country without a visa, in a display of Islamic solidarity.

From 1992 on, the U.S. alleges that bin Laden and other al Qaeda members decided that the group should set aside its differences with other Shiite Muslim terrorist organizations in order to cooperate against the perceived common enemy, the United States and its allies. U.S. authorities say the targets of these attacks included U.S. military forces in Saudi Arabia and in Yemen and U.S. forces stationed in the Horn of Africa, including Somalia.
In October 1993, as part of the U.S. humanitarian relief effort in Somalia, 18 U.S. servicemen were killed during an operation in Mogadishu. Their bodies were dragged through the streets. In a 1997 interview with CNN, bin Laden said his followers, together with local Muslims, killed those troops.

U.S. law enforcement also alleges that bin Laden has ties to failed attacks on two hotels in Yemen where U.S. troops stayed en route to Somalia.

In 1994, the Saudi government revoked bin Laden's citizenship and froze his assets in Saudi Arabia because of his support for Muslim fundamentalist movements.

In 1996, bin Laden issued a "declaration of jihad," writing that his goal is to drive the U.S. military out of Saudi Arabia and overthrow the Saudi government.

The Most Wanted List

The U.S. government has offered a $5 million reward for information leading to bin Laden's arrest, while it also works through diplomatic channels to pressure the Taliban government in Afghanistan to hand over the fugitive millionaire.

In 1999, the U.S. won approval from the U.N. Security Council for limited economic sanctions against the Taliban and in late 2000 stepped up the pressure when the U.S. and Russia pushed through an arms embargo against Afghanistan.

The U.S. had alleged that bin Laden was linked with a number of terrorist incidents aimed at the U.S., including the World Trade Center bombing.

On June 8, 1998, bin Laden was indicted in New York City on one count of conspiracy to attack U.S. defense installations. The indictment alleges that bin Laden's al Qaeda organization trained and assisted the Somali tribesmen who killed U.S. soldiers in October 1993.

But bin Laden is most wanted for his alleged involvement in the African embassy bombings, which happened two months after his initial indictment by U.S. authorities.

On August 7, 1998, the eighth anniversary of both the approval of U.N. sanctions against Iraq and the order made by President George Bush to send U.S. troops to the Gulf, two truck bombs were detonated at the U.S. embassies in Nairobi, Kenya, and Dar es Salaam, Tanzania. The Nairobi explosion killed 213 people and injured more than 4,500 while 11 people were killed and 85 injured in the Dar es Salaam bombing.

Most of the victims were Africans, including some who were Muslim. But bin Laden said, in an interview he gave to TIME magazine in late 1998 that was published in January 1999, that he understood the "motives of the brothers who act against the enemies of the nation.

"When it becomes apparent that it would be impossible to repel these Americans without assaulting them, even if this involved the killing of Muslims, this is permissible under Islam," he said.

"Our job is to instigate"

He was careful not to take responsibility for the African embassy bombings in the TIME interview, saying only that "our job is to instigate and, by the grace of God, we did that -- and certain people responded to this instigation."

The United States responded differently as it believes bin Laden was the mastermind behind the embassy bombings. Fourteen days later, on August 20, 1998, President Bill Clinton ordered cruise missile attacks against suspected terrorist training camps in Afghanistan and a pharmaceutical plant in Khartoum, Sudan. But one of the targets provoked much controversy. U.S. intelligence officials claimed that the Sudanese pharmaceutical plant was helping bin Laden produce chemical weapons, which was angrily denied by the Sudanese government. The attack wounded seven civilians, one of whom later died.

In September 1998, U.S. officials admitted to The New York Times that the U.S. had no evidence that directly linked bin Laden to the Khartoum plant. But intelligence officials said there were financial transactions between bin Laden and Military Industrial Corp., run by the Sudanese government. In addition, the U.S. said a soil sample taken near the plant included a chemical that is a precursor to the deadly nerve gas VX.

Trial underway of four accused

The indictment against bin Laden charges him with engaging in a conspiracy to murder American citizens and with concealing the activities of his co-conspirators by, among other things, establishing "front" companies, providing false identity and travel documents, engaging in coded correspondence and providing false information to authorities in various countries.

And while bin Laden remains at-large in Afghanistan, protected by the Taliban who control the country, others have been arrested for the embassy bombings. Of the 22 people indicted in connection with the bombings, four men are on trial in a federal court in New York City. Jury selection began on January 3 in the conspiracy trial of Wadih el Hage (alleged to be bin Laden's personal secretary), Khalfan Khamis Mohamed, Mohamed Rashed Daoud al 'Owhali and Mohammed Sadeek Odeh.

On October 20, 2000, Ali Mohamed, a U.S. citizen and another man named in the indictment, pleaded guilty to the five broad conspiracy charges against him. Mohamed, a bin Laden confidante, admitted staking out several possible U.S. targets, including the Nairobi embassy. He has been cooperating with the government and is expected to be called as a key witness.

Another defendant is in U.S. custody and three others are in the United Kingdom awaiting extradition. Thirteen others, including bin Laden and the top leadership of his al Qaeda organization, remain fugitives.

CNN Executive Producer Nancy Peckenham and CNN Terrorism Analyst Peter Bergen contributed to this report, written by CNN.com writer/editor Douglas S. Wood.

Violence

Violence. Violence. We see everywhere and every day.

You get up in the morning. Make a cup of coffee or tea. Turn the local television or the radio on for the early morning news. What do you hear most of the time? Invariably, we hear about the robbery, or murder, or arson, or gang fight and violence that happened overnight in your own neighborhood. As you get ready to go to work or to get the kids ready for the school, the local TV switches on to its affiliated respective national network channel (ABC, CBS, NBC, FOX, etc.) for the national news. The national network channels, amongst other things, will invariably convey similar unpleasant stories on violence that occurred on national level and in countries like Middle East. Lunchtime news is no different. It may even sometime bring the news about the bullies in the school bus or violent incidents like what happened in the Columbine shootings, or some sort of the hostage and shooting incidents in the workplace, etc.

Okay, you finished your day at work and got back home for the day. What sort of evening entertainment do you get? Have you given violent video games to your kids? Do you like to watch violent sports programs like the professional wrestling, boxing or football; or movies like *Pulp Fiction*, *Scream*, *Natural Born Killers'*, etc. most of the time? You have no problem. You can find plenty of that type of violent entertainment on the TV screen or in the neighborhood movie screen.

What is wrong with our society? Aren't we supposed to be civilized, loving, caring and sharing type of people? While I was working in Saudi Arabia, and when my family and I were traveling in Singapore and Malaysia, we had no such fear of having to subject ourselves or witness any such violent acts or crimes. Of course, we had other type of worries like appalling driving conditions in Saudi Arabia at that time. Believe it or not, in those days, the Saudis stopped **sometimes** when they see the red lights at the road junctions.

Who are these evil elements that commit these acts of violence and crimes? Why do they commit all these atrocities? **Almost in all these acts of violence and crime we see one common factor: the use of guns in some form or other.**

It is extremely difficult to do an in depth analysis on each and every type of the acts of violence and crimes. But, let us have an overall view of this unpleasant episode and see whether we can make any sense out of it.

As briefed in the chapter "War on Terror," these local terrorists live in your own neighborhood. Except for a few cases like the offenders in the Columbine shooting incident, most of these young thugs are from broken or unstable families. Most of these kids from the single parent families or from the families where parents bicker frequently invariably tend to have unsecured feelings about their future and their lives every day. In some of these cases, the offenders are the victims of constant bullying in the schools.

In view of this type of family background and atmosphere in the schools, most of these kids don't do well with their studies at school, but instead tend to get into all types of undesirable mischief and acts of violence like becoming gang member. In all fairness to these kids, it is not their fault. We, the parents, should take full responsibility in this context. Whether it is deliberate or not, we drove them towards this type of appalling and undesirable path of acts of violence and crime.

The kids at that early age are like the wet clay. They don't know the rights from wrongs. The peer pressures very easily persuade them to get into all sorts of unwanted mischief. We, the parents, must remember this. We can shape the wet clay into either an angel or a monster. It is we, the parents, who brought them into existence. If we are not mentally matured enough to bring them up properly, showering our sustained love and care, teaching them the virtues and values of good life in a society followed by persistent monitoring of their day-to-day activities and actual behaviour, then we should not have had the children. Under these unfortunate circumstances, whether we like to admit or not, we are nothing but real unfit and irresponsible parents. No useful purpose will be served by trying to find excuses in this respect.

If your kid turned out to be a big bully terrorizing other kids, then it is your fault. If your kid is roaming around the neighborhood late in the nights instead of being in bed after consolidating what he/she studied in the school that day, then it is your fault. If your child is a member of a gang in your neighborhood, then it is your fault. I can go on and on like this on this issue. The main point I am trying to emphasize here is that we, the parents, are responsible in respect of how our kids turn out to be.

If we are really the loving, caring and sharing type of parents and if our kids do perceive us as such, they will look on us as their real role models. In turn, eventually, they also will turn out to be good as well.

Okay, we all know that prevention is better than the cure. There is no use in you **just** telling the child that you love and care about that child. Of course, you have to repeatedly tell them also. What I am trying to say is that he/she must realize and be convinced at all times that he/she is loved and cared for by you. They need your emotional and physical support at all times. Assuming that your child is not spoiled yet, we can do the following hopefully to make them as good citizens:

- Try and spend as much of time as possible with your child.
- Be not only a parent but also a real good friend so that the child feels comfortable to confide anything and everything that he/she wants to share with.
- Help with the school homework, but don't do it for them.
- Constantly communicate with your child.
- Don't give them or encourage them to watch violent TV programs or video games.
- Watch with them good inspiring movies like *Guess who is coming for dinner* but definitely not the violent and vulgar movies like *Pulp Fiction*.
- If you are interested in watching any of the "R" and "X" rated movies or documentaries, then do so when they are not around.
- Besides the school background, children pick up foul languages from the movies. Since they are very susceptible for anything at that age, they think it is "cool" to talk and behave like those characters in the movies.
- Remember the saying, "tell me about your friends, then I will tell you about you'. So, keep an eye on the type of friends your child has and move with.

• Encourage them to read a lot of biographies and autobiographies of legends like Mahatma Gandhi, Dr. Martin Luther King, Nelson Mandela, etc. etc., just to name a few that I know of.

• Encourage them to read a lot of inspiring books that will give them good guiding principles for a bright and better future.

• Encourage them to read Dale Carnegie's books like *How to Stop Worrying and Start Living*, that shows the practical way to overcome fears and anxieties in our day-to-day lives; and *How to Win Friends and Influence People*, that shows how to effectively get along with every one in our lives. These two books are excellent practical guides which, when really put into practice will lead to a real happy and good life.

• Encourage them to get interested in games like basketball, soccer, etc. If you can afford, also encourage them to participate in tennis, golf, etc.

• Encourage them to get interested in arts, music, dancing etc.

• Keep them fully active and occupied both mentally and physically at all times.

• Be in close contact with your child's teacher to find out how the child is behaving and performing in the school. A child's character is moulded based on how good you and the teacher work towards it.

• Encourage the child to be creative and find out what his/her real interests and aspirations are. Check them out and encourage them to pursue them, if they are towards his/her better future.

• Make them realize the danger involved in using drugs, cigarettes, etc.

• Motivate and encourage the children to go to the places of worship. But, never ever let the children believe in violence as the means to get whatever they may want. Remember what is happening in the Middle East, Northern Island, India and Pakistan. Violence should never be a part of your religious faith.

There are numerous things that one can list in this respect. But, you know the child better than anyone else. So, if need be, get advice from others and do whatever you can come up with to motivate your child for a better future. First of all, you must be good since the children normally try to copy the parents.

I know that I will get told off and will be asked to get lost when I say this. Letting the children to watch extreme sports and violent programs like professional wrestling, boxing, and American football / Commonwealth rugby game will invariably turn the child to become violent without their knowing. Because, at that age all they try to do is just imitate and copy what they see on the screen. They don't know any better. They don't realize that they are committing a serious and dangerous act when they embark on their imitation and copying.

You don't have to take my word for it. If you don't believe me, please checkout the following site:

http://www.cbsnews.com/stories/2001/03/09/national/main277536.shtml.

Under the heading *"Wrestling" Case Draws Life Sentence,* the site states the following:

"A boy who says he was imitating body-slamming pro wrestlers when he killed a little girl at age 12 was sentenced to life in prison without parole Friday after a judge refused to reduce his first-degree murder conviction."

Beside, please never ever expose your child to any movie or documentary that has nothing but foul language and violence. Children when exposed to these programs, invariably tend to think that it is "cool" to use the rude words and also to imitate the characters. As per the site, *http://www.eurekalert.org/ pub_releases/2002-12/dc-sft121902.php,*

"Parents need to do a better job of monitoring children's access to movies. Parents wouldn't think of exposing their children to food with arsenic in it. We need to teach them to think of violent movies in the same way,"

Okay, in spite of all your sincere efforts or perhaps because you left it too late, your child might have turned out to be not the way you wished, but as the one involved in violent activities and crimes. It is unfortunate. But, still you have to do your best to try to get it right. I mentioned in the initial section of the chapter "War on Terror" some of the possible preferred course of actions that you as parent can take in the interest of your child and your community. Just for completeness of this chapter and also for ready reference herein, let me brief the contents of that section below.

Find the best possible time when your child can be receptive to speak with you on whatever you may have to say. At that appropriate time try and have a real good chat with your child explaining the eventual consequences of his/her violent and criminal activities. Put everything in a nice and pleasant way, but not in an accusing manner.

Hopefully, after your close, intimate conversation, if you are lucky, the child may realize the dangers involved in the path being pursued and may try and avoid following that path in future. It would be wonderful, if it happens.

But, at the same time, the chances are he/she may not listen to your advice, let whatever be the reason, and change his/her behavior. In that case, in the interest of everyone around you, especially your child, please consider the following remedial course of actions.

Give an ultimatum to your child to the effect that, if he/she refuses to stop the criminal activities, you would contact the local law enforcing people. Then, hope and pray that it works.

If there is no change in his/her behavior, then do contact the police. I know that it is easier said than done. Your child or the gang concerned may intimidate and threaten you in this context. But, please think it over, what is the alternative? If you don't do anything positive to stop this, then your neighbor or even you may be the next victim and your child eventually will get rounded up for serious crime and even may get shot or killed. Sure, you don't want this serious situation to happen to anyone including your child and your community. So, please do something positive in the interest of all concerned. It is unfortunate. But, you have to deal with it in a positive way. There is no use in you just keeping quiet hoping that he/she will behave better soon. It won't happen. You need to take positive action. There are no two ways about it.

Contact your local, state and federal lawmakers insisting that relevant appropriate legislative action must be effected immediately to minimize and eventually eliminate this problem of violence in the society for good. Presently the laws seem to be more lenient towards the offenders. No body seems to give serious consideration to the innocent victim's rights? This should be the primary concern for every body. Innocent people must be protected at all cost first. Request your lawmakers and government officials to explore and implement laws that will

- Monitor the movement of the known offenders,
- Round up the offender on the first act of violence, and
- Send them to the boot camps (Correctional facilities that use the training techniques applied to military recruits to teach the offenders socially acceptable patterns of behaviors) and keep them there until such time these offenders are rehabilitated as caring citizens acceptable to the community.

We get the usual story saying that they haven't got enough resources to fund for more law enforcing personnel, jails, boot camps, etc. Then, tell those guys whose main responsibility is to provide protection for us to find resources immediately. **There is nothing more important than our right to live in our own community free from the fear of robbery, rape, vandalism, murder, gang violence, and drive by shooting, etc.** Insist that they have to get this issue as one of their top most priority items to resolve successfully at the earliest possible time. You need to constantly pester your local lawmakers and government officials until a working solution is found for this serious menace in your community.

As mentioned before, guns seems to be a common factor invariably in every instance of violence and crime. It is sad and unfortunate that gun culture is so deep rooted in the hearts and minds of most of the Americans. In effect most of the Americans are brainwashed in this respect. I know of quite a number of my colleagues who are very decent, well educated and just leading a normal good life like anybody else, but have an obsession for buying and hoarding guns at their homes. In some cases, they did have some fatal accidents where the kids messed around with the guns. Of course, they were shocked and sad that this accident happened. But, still they would not get rid of the guns from their homes. I can't believe it. But, it is the sad state of affairs. For generations these families were brought up in gun culture and as such fully brainwashed.

Then, there is the Constitutional provision regarding the right to own firearms. As per the website, *http://news.bbc.co.uk/1/low/world/americas/ 725614.stm,*

"The right to own a firearm is embedded in the American psyche like a splinter of flint, jagged and immovable.

It all goes back to the Founding Fathers who in 1791 amended the new American constitution with the following words: 'A well regulated militia, being necessary to the security of a free state, the right of the people to keep and bear arms, shall not be infringed.'

This amendment was drawn up by people living in a precarious agrarian society unrecognizable to modern Americans, when communities needed guns to hunt and to protect themselves from Indians and highwaymen.

The gun lobby has plucked out the phrase "the right of the people to keep and bear arms" and used it ever since to beat down every serious attempt at gun control in America by claiming a violation of the constitution."

There is no need to document herein the details of gun violence. All you need to do is just turn on your television for the news. There are quite a lot of reports regarding gun violence. Have you seen the documentary film, *Bowling for Columbine* that won an Oscar award? This film is a real big eye-opener for the people who believe in and practice common sense in their day-to-day life, but definitely not for the people who are incurably brainwashed with American gun culture.

Most of the Republicans and selected few democrats support the activities of the National Rifle Association. Please checkout the website *http:// w w w . o p e n s e c r e t s . o r g / o v e r v i e w / topcontribs.asp?Bkdn=DemRep&Cycle=2004* for a list of "TOP DONORS." There have been numerous attempts to have an effective gun control laws. Since the National Rifle Association has a very powerful ally in both the Executive and Legislative branch of the American government, God only can save this country from the clutches of these gun maniacs.

I am not advocating for any gun control law. I am all for gun eradication from the hands of every ordinary civilian. I know for certain that I am going to get shouted at or even shot at for saying this. But, the purpose of this book is to share my thoughts and views with you, the readers. You may not like it or approve of what I say. But, as you can appreciate, I am entitled to express my views and thoughts. So, here I go.

I truly believe in our God Almighty. I believe in the philosophy that Mahatma Gandhi used. As such, **whenever any injustice is inflicted on the innocent people, I would like everyone to stand up and fight in a peaceful way to rectify the situation. Non-violence and non-cooperation should be our tools, but not the guns.** Please don't forget this history. Early settlers of America got rid of the British from America through civil war and blood bath. How did the "half-naked fakir" (Mahatma Gandhi) get rid of the British Empire from India? He rallied the people behind him and used peaceful, persistent, non-violent and non-cooperative activities as his weapons. He made the entirety of India stand still through this type of movement. As such, the British authorities had no other alternative except to pack up their bags and leave India for good. Remember, no violence or any gun was used in this peaceful movement by the people even though they were hurt and subjected to the guns and violent activities by the British. As such, the following are my views.

The constitutional provision regarding "the right to bear arms" is outdated and not appropriate for the present-day modern America. As such, this provision should be scrapped in view of the numbers of the deaths where guns were involved.

Every effort must be made to confiscate and destroy every gun from every civilian. No civilian should keep or use any gun. Only law enforcing officials should be allowed to carry gun **while they are on duty** and use it only when it is absolutely necessary.

Honestly, please tell me why any civilian should own or use any gun?

I hear at least two arguments trying to justify for possessing and using guns.

One argument is, for self-protection. My question then is this. If every civilian is prohibited from having or using a gun, then you need protection from whom?

The other argument is, for hunting. Is hunting your hobby? Why do you want a hobby to go and kill those innocent animals and birds? What did they do to you? If you are concerned about, perhaps, the over population of any of those animals or birds and any of them becoming a real menace and nuisance to you at your backyard, then why can't you leave this issue in the hands of the professionals from the humane society? They can hunt them down. **If you insist that you want to hang on to this hunting habit, then tell me this. In this case, in what way you are any better than any of those gang members and those thugs who enjoy drive by shooting?** I rest my arguments here.

———————————

Points for *Something To Think About*:

- Violence. Violence. We see everywhere and every day.
- Almost every act of violence and crime involves the use of guns.
- Most of these offenders are from broken or unstable families.
- Some of these offenders are the victims of constant bullying.
- The parents are responsible for how their kids turn out to be.
- If we are not capable of bringing up our kids properly, then we should not have had the children. We are unfit to be parents.
- If we, the parents, are really loving, caring and sharing parents and are perceived as real good role models to our kids, then our kids will turn out to be good as well.
- Prevention is better than cure. So, do all you can to prevent your child getting involved with any violent acts or gangs.
- Check out the section above regarding what the parents can do to prevent the children getting involved with violence.
- The children must realize and be convinced that they are loved and cared for by you, the parent, at all times. They need your emotional and physical support at all times.
- Letting the children to watch extreme sports and violent programs like professional wrestling, boxing, and American football / Commonwealth rugby game will turn the child to become violent without their knowing.
- Never ever expose your child to any movie or documentary that has nothing but foul language and violence.
- At an early age, children try to imitate and copy whatever they see on

the screen. This includes rude and foul language and violent acts.

• There is nothing more important than our right to live in our own community free from the fear of robbery, rape, vandalism, murder, gang violence, and drive by shooting, etc.

• Gun seems to be a common factor invariably in every violence activity and crime.

• American gun culture is deep rooted in the hearts and minds of most of the Americans. As such, they have an obsession for buying and hoarding guns at their homes. For generations these families were brought up in gun culture and as such fully brainwashed.

• The National Rifle Association has very powerful allies in the both the Executive and Legislative branch of the American government.

• The constitutional provision regarding "the right to bear arms" is outdated and not appropriate for the present-day modern America. As such should be scrapped in view of the number of the deaths where guns were involved.

• Every effort must be made to confiscate and destroy every gun from every civilian.

• No civilian should keep or use any gun. Only law enforcing officials should be allowed to carry gun while they are on duty and use it only when it is absolutely necessary.

• If you want to enjoy hunting the animals and birds using the guns, then you are no better than those gang members and thugs who enjoy killing innocent people through "drive by shooting."

Media

As briefed before in the "Introduction" chapter, the media is the most powerful means for communication, education and entertainment. When I say education, I am talking about **educating the people with all the facts** on what is going on in the community, country and the world at large.

Media is a means of mass communication through television, radio, newspaper, movies, magazines, journals, books, flyers (pamphlets or circulars for mass distribution), etc. According to me, it should be an industry or an establishment, where a group of investigative journalists and others collect all the facts that concern the well being of the people at large, and present those facts without any fabrication or bias for the people to see, listen, and read. This will help the people to make their own considered judgement of what is happening around them. This is extremely important for the people to know the facts.

Presenting the facts without any fabrication may not be that important for the media owners, since their only concern is how to make more and more profit at any cost and by whatever means they can. Ordinary people do not have access or means or time to collect all the facts that concern them. This is where the media has a major role to play by educating the people. This helps to ensure proper functioning of the democracy. The media can effectively make or break the true image of a person or a society or a country depending on how they present the facts.

Do you really believe everything that is presented to you by the media? I used to believe it, but not anymore. There were numerous instances when I happened to witness what the reporters were reporting which were in no way close to the real situation that I saw for myself. So, what does this mean? The facts are there somewhere. The reporter collects the information to the best he/she can and then **conveys the information the way he/she wants to present** to the public. What percentage of the facts did we get in relation to the reality is anybody's guess. As an example, *http://worldfilm.about.com/ cs/documentarie1/fr/controlroom_p.htm* gives a review on a documentary film *Control Room*. Please check this site out. It shows clearly how the "facts" related to the Iraq war are being presented by the media owners in different ways to the audience. The account of what is happening in Iraq war by Al Jazeera, the largest Arab News Network, is very much different to what we in the West witness on our television.

So, what to believe and whom to believe? God only knows. But, at the same time having said that, what other choice do we, the ordinary people, have to know the facts? None. We need to and want to know the facts. But, the unfortunate reality at the moment is, we have to take whatever we can find from the media, mostly with a pinch of salt.

Media world is a highly competitive business. The media needs to use all the available latest technologies and resources to collect and present the information as soon as possible in the best way possible. I truly admire and respect all the people who work in the media world. Most of these people are highly skilled, talented and dedicated to collect and present the facts to the best they can. Left to themselves they will do a great job of presenting the facts without any fabrication. Mr. Peter Arnett, the legend in the field of journalism, is just an example in this context. The honest and factual presentation will help to promote proper functioning of the democracy. This can happen, if and only if there is no interference from programs' managers who are controlled by the media owners. This is where I have major grievance with the media owners. We are all aware of what happened to Peter Arnett who was sacked by NBC for "telling the truth" which unfortunately happen to be politically incorrect and not the way Bush Administration would like.

Who are these media owners? Any Tom, Dick and Harry like you and me cannot be a media owner. This is a very big and powerful industry. It needs quite a lot of skilled and dedicated human resources and high tech equipments to be used in every pivotal corner of the world. This, in turn, means that a lot of money is required to run this business. As such, only those few people who can afford to dedicate their time and invest whatever they may have or those big corporations who can afford to make quite a big investment can really embark on this business.

As an example for one of the dedicated private people in the media world, I can think of Mr. Michael Moore, the author of a number of books including best sellers (*Adventures in a TV Nation, Downsize This, Stupid White* Men, and *Dude, Where's My Country?*) and the director and producer of a number of documentary films including Oscar Award winning film (*The Awful Truth, TV Nation, Roger & Me, Bowling for Columbine,* and *Fahrenheit 9/11"* that I know of. I salute him for the noble services he is providing to the ordinary citizens of the world. In my opinion, he is simply the best. Because, like what I am trying to do now, his ultimate aim, all along has been, to educate the innocent people who are ignorant of what is going on around them. He exposes the evil doings of the dirty politicians and greedy corporations.

But, here there is one unfortunate reality. His work and publications will have only limited exposure to the public at large as compared to the exposure that the public would get from the network radios and televisions like ABC, CBS, NBC, PBS, FOX, etc. It would be a real big blessing to the ordinary people, if only dedicated people like him can join together with other rich people who have sufficient money to open a new network channel **AND** who have similar passion and determination to educate the people. I'm sure there are quite a number of websites that are dedicated to educate everyone. I list below just a few that I know of. No particular significance or importance is attached as regards to the sequence of this listing. This is just a list.

http://www.michaelmoore.com/
http://www.brillig.com/debt_clock/
http://www.us-democratorship.com/
http://www.moveon.org/
http://www.alternet.org/
http://www.dissidentvoice.org/
http://www.carnegieendowment.org/
http://www.truthout.org/
http://www.tompaine.com/
http://www.americanprogress.org/
http://www.freespeech.org/
http://www.prisonplanet.com/
http://www.cryptome.org/
http://oldamericancentury.org/
http://www.consortiumnews.com/

http://www.whodies.com/
http://www.truthaboutwar.org/
http://www.ericblumrich.com/
http://www.gregpalast.com/
http://www.thenation.com/
http://bernie.house.gov/
http://www.opensecrets.org/
http://www-tech.mit.edu/

But, the problem here is, how many ordinary citizens are likely to have access to the Internet or know-how to browse through these sites on the Internet? From poor peoples' point of view, we need a simple, easy to access inexpensive means of media like a nationwide network radio and television similar to ABC, CBS, NBC, FOX, etc. If only any of these network channels can make a sincere effort to educate the people properly by providing all the facts that the people need to know in the interest of proper functioning of the democracy, then there is no problem. But, unfortunately, these networks are very hesitant and reluctant to provide the facts that may not be acceptable to the media owner since it may not be acceptable to the government of the day.

For example, in the case of Peter Arnett, as per *http://news.bbc.co.uk/2/ hi/americas/2903503.stm,*

"Iraqi television broadcast him saying, 'the first war plan has just failed because of Iraqi resistance. Clearly the American war planners misjudged the determination of the Iraqi forces.'"

He was fired by the NBC since he made these politically incorrect statements.

As per, *http://www.us-democratorship.com/links.htm*

"A completely different view on the Iraq war. ABC, CBS, NBC, CNN and Fox News are all competing to get the largest market share in the USA by presenting a "comfortable" view on the war, that the typical American patriot wants to see during his breakfast or lunch hour or as his "evening entertainment." Fox News is probably the most "patriotic" of those News services. For Europeans like me often disgusting to see, but unfortunately reality. This is modern war propaganda in the year 2003. They spoon-feed America with all the thin arguments the Bush administration could find to justify this war."

Also, please checkout the site *http://www.dissidentvoice.org/Feb04/ Petersen0202.htm*. This link gives most valuable information in respect of *"The Awesome Destructive Power of the Corporate Power Media."* In view of this, since I very much want the people to know, at least now, what we normally don't get to know, I have copied the entire report at the end of this chapter. I hope that you, the reader, would please care to check it out. It is an eye opener.

The following few sections, presented **as given in the source**, are very important to note and remember forever. Besides, it is also the reason behind what I intend to state subsequently:

"Howard Dean has joined the list of victims of U.S. corporate media consolidation. Dean shares this distinction with <u>Dennis Kucinich</u> and the people of the formerly sovereign state of Iraq, among many others. Dean was stripped of <u>half</u> his popular support in the space of two weeks in January while John Kerry—who tied in the polls with Carol Moseley-Braun at seven percent just <u>two months</u> earlier—rose like a genie from a bottle to become the overnight presidential frontrunner. Both candidates were shocked and disoriented by the dizzying turns of fortune, and for good reason. Neither Dean nor Kerry had done anything on their own that could have so dramatically altered the race. Corporate America decided that Dean must be savaged, and its media sector made it happen.

This commentary, however, is not about the <u>merits of Howard Dean</u>. If a mildly progressive, Internet-driven, young, white middle class-centered, campaign such as Dean's—flush with money derived from unconventional sources, backed by significant sections of labor, reinforced by big name endorsements and surging with upward momentum—can be derailed in a matter of weeks at the whim of corporate media, then all of us are in deep trouble. The Dean beat-down should signal an intense reassessment of media's role in the American power structure. The African-American historical experience has much to offer in that regard, since the Civil Rights and Black Power Movements were born in a wrestling match with an essentially hostile corporate (white) media. However, there can be no meaningful discussion of the options available to progressive forces in the United States unless it is first recognized that the corporate media in the current era is the enemy, and must be treated that way.

Media companies act in effective unison on matters of importance to the larger corporate class. For all politically useful purposes, the monopolization of US media is now complete, in that the corporate owners and managers of the dominant organs are interchangeable and indistinguishable, sharing a common mission and world view. (That's the underlying reason why their "news" product is nearly identical.)"

"Media rushed to embed themselves in the US war machine's Iraq invasion, and collaborated to actively suppress public awareness of a full-blown movement against the war. Hundreds of thousands of protestors were made to <u>disappear</u> in plain sight."

"Corporate media's ties to the Pirates in Washington are organic and nearly seamless."

"The media giants subjected Clinton to the full fury of the Hard Right's campaign to destabilize his presidency, ultimately resulting in impeachment hearings."

"Clinton's Republican predecessors were not subjected to anything approaching such scrutiny and abuse. It is self-evident that George Bush, who should have been buried under a glacier of scandal and criminality within months of entering the White House, enjoys the full-time protection of the corporate press. Their institutional intention is to elect him again. Media apologists offer fictions about press vs. power, when in reality corporate media = corporate power, just as Bush = corporate power. The Democrats are not part of this equation."

"Howard Dean's brilliant use of the Internet allowed him to capitalize on anti-war sentiment while assembling a funding base independent of the usual corporate suspects. Dean's <u>December surge</u> took the corporate media by surprise, alarming the bosses and their friends in the White House. Like a Mormon Tabernacle Choir, the corporate media rose with one voice to question Dean's "electability." It is important to note that in mid-December, according to _Newsweek's poll_, Dean, Kerry and Clark were doing equally in a match-up with George Bush, at 40, 41, and 41 percent, respectively. There was no statistical basis to single out Dean as unelectable. Dean had just gotten the endorsement of Al Gore and two of the nation's most important unions, AFSCME and SEIU. No matter. The corporate media has the power of self-fulfilling prophesy, and they know it. Negative impressions rained down on Dean like a monsoon, and didn't let up even after the damage was done. Dean was tagged by the media as a loser to Bush well before he let out "The Scream"—an innocuous, non-event, on the night of his Iowa defeat."

"In order to reduce the increasing control of the Political Opinion Complex over our political process, we need to begin developing and strengthening institutions strong enough to counter its current influence. Specifically, we need to further develop networks where political information can be mass distributed outside of the POC's control. Not long ago, there were several such outside institutions. Unions and churches were a far more pervasive part of people's lives. Newspapers and periodicals were significantly more numerous and varied in their political outlook. Public television and radio had far larger audiences. Political parties and societies were either machines or at least overflowing with active members. All of these now weakened institutions once served as means to perform end-runs outside the control of the corporate media and the Political Opinion Complex. Engagement with the political process through means other than television was far greater. However, those institutions no longer serve as significant counter-weights to the strength of the Political Opinion Complex."

"There is no question that Blacks and progressives must establish alternative media outlets, and not just on the Internet. However, there is no substitute for confronting the corporate media head-on, through direct mass action and other, creative tactics. The rich men's voices must be de-legitimized in the eyes of the people, who already suspect that we are being systematically lied to and manipulated. African-Americans have an advantage in this regard, since they are used to being lied to and about.
No society in human history has confronted an enemy as omnipresent as the US corporate media. Yet there is no choice but to challenge their hegemony."

So, I very much request all these investigative reporters of these various websites to explore the possibilities of joining together, along with some rich people who have similar devotion to educate people, to initiate a new nationwide radio and television networks. Ultimate aim of this new network should be to collect and convey the facts that every citizen must know in the interest of the proper functioning of the democracy. Both the religious and political extremists don't need this type of service. This new service is needed for the category of the people who are known as "the middle of the road" or "the swing voters." These are the people who are going to decide the fate of any country. But, unfortunately, they don't get the required unbiased education on current affairs and present day politics at the moment. As such they are unable to make a considered decision accordingly in respect of whom to elect.

As we all know, every media is very much interested in making money and hence they are actively competing against each other to get the best possible rating at all times. Excellent rating means more money through more media commercial advertisements. Nobody blames anyone on this count. **The media must realize that its first and foremost duty must be to serve the people by providing all the information that the people should know for proper functioning of the democracy. This is because, it is the people who enable the media to get the desired rating and hence the money. So, they have moral obligation to do this to the people first.** This is where I have my main grievance with the media. The media can collect and present the information that concerns the people and still get very good ratings and more money. Let me cite some instances in this context.

Katherine Harris was the Florida's Secretary of State in charge of the elections in Florida **AND** Head of the Bush election campaign in Florida. Obviously, there is a real good conflict of interest here. In the interest of the democracy, the media should have alerted the people well in advance explaining in detail the impact of this situation. This would have given the media very good rating since everyone would be anxious to get to know the danger of this situation. But, the media did not do this.

Well in advance as preparation for the election in 2000, the Republican controlled Florida State legislature made a law in 1998 to the effect that ex-felons cannot vote in Florida. This means that 31 % of all black men in

Florida who are likely to vote for democrats would be prohibited from voting. The media could have warned the people nationwide, well in advance, explaining in detail the impact of this on the democracy. This would have given them good coverage and hence the rating. But, the media did not do this.

Katherine Harris did everything in her power to eliminate a lot of eligible voters who are likely to vote for democrats and also tried her best to stop recounting the suspicious votes. In the interest of the democracy, the media could have given more nationwide coverage explaining in detail the consequence of her actions. But, the media did not do this.

The media could have given wider coverage of the injustice inflicted on the democracy by those five Supreme Court Justices and earned more money. But, the media did not do this.

Almost the entire world population, including Pope John Paul II, *http:// www.globalexchange.org/countries/iraq/522.html*, was opposed to the Iraq invasion by USA. The media could have explained in detail and at length to the entire nation the consequences of this illegal and immoral invasion and earned better rating. Again, the media could have given wider coverage of the anti-war protest. But, the media did not do this. Instead the media became the mouthpiece for the warmongers.

During the period when the republicans spent so much of taxpayers' money and valuable legislative time to derail Clintons, the media, in the interest of democracy, could have alerted the citizens the danger of the personal vendetta by the republicans. But, the media did not do this.

Even now, the media could have given wider coverage of the peaceful protests by the people who are opposed to Bush's policy instead of covering only the Bush's supporters and earned more money. But, the media did not do this.

I can go on and on in this respect. If making more money were the only object, then the media would have done this. But, the media's real objective is primarily something else and it is to ensure that corporate interests are protected and provided at any cost and by any means. Who will meet the corporate interests? Of course, it will be the republicans, only the republicans, and none other than republicans. So, the corporate media, whether it is ABC or CBS or NBC or FOX or CNN doesn't matter, in their own subtle way they continue to do every thing they can to keep the republicans at the helm. Media can do so much to enrich and ensure real democracy, if only they serve the people instead of stabbing them after earning money through them. The media wants the government to serve the interests of the greedy corporations, but not the interests of the people who elect the government. This is the tragedy.

The rich people and the right-wingers control almost all the present media sources. They know all the best ways on how to fool the people and still make money through them. They are very good at it and well experienced in this respect.

So, what can we, the ordinary people, do about this? I can think of just four possible solutions.

1.   Insist to ensure that the lawmakers make appropriate laws to institute a new network very similar to BBC of the United Kingdom **funded by the people's money to serve the people's interests**, but not the corporate interests. Please checkout the website http://www.bbc.co.uk/cgi-bin/ education/betsie/parser.pl for the information on how the BBC is run.

2.   Appeal to the conscience of the corporate media to serve the people first by providing all the information needed for proper functioning of the democracy, while they make money using the people.

3.   Appeal to all those investigative reporters who work with various cited websites to explore the possibility of joining together to initiate a new people oriented network media like BBC of the United Kingdom.

4.   I know that this is extremely difficult since big corporations control almost all the networks in the USA. But, we have to checkout out to find out which one to trust and then watch that media source only. For example, I do not watch NBC and MSNBC anymore, ever since Peter Arnett was fired by NBC. I look elsewhere for reasonably fair presentation of the facts that concern the people. **If people can turn to only those media**

outlets, which hopefully serve the people at least to some extent, then there may be a chance for the corporate media to correct the current attitude of serving the corporate interests first.

Points for *Something To Think About*:

- Media's main role should be to educate everyone with all the facts related to proper functioning of the democracy.
- The media can make or break the true image of a person or a society or a country depending on how they present facts, if they want to present the facts.
- People need to and want to know the facts. But, the unfortunate reality at the moment is, we have no other alternative except to take whatever we can get from the corporate media, mostly with a pinch of salt.
- As in the case of Peter Arnett, left to themselves the investigative journalists will do a marvelous job of presenting the facts without any fabrication. But, there is constant interference from programs' managers who are controlled by the media owners.
- There are quite a few websites that are dedicated to educate everyone with facts. Some are listed above. But, not everyone is computer literate and has access to computer. So, we need simple, easy to access inexpensive means of nationwide network radio and television to know the facts.
- Howard Dean is the victim of U.S. corporate media consolidation. Corporate America decided that Dean must be savaged, and its media sector made it happen. If Dean's upward momentum can be derailed in a matter of weeks at the whim of corporate media, then all of us are in deep trouble. The Dean beat-down should signal an intense reassessment of media's role in the US power structure.
- The media giants subjected Clinton to the full fury of the Hard Right's campaign to destabilize his presidency, ultimately resulting in impeachment hearings. Don't forget the amount of taxpayers' money and legislative time wasted in this respect.
- "In order to reduce the increasing control of the Political Opinion Complex over our political process, we need to begin developing and strengthening institutions strong enough to counter its current influence.

Specifically, we need to further develop networks where political information can be mass distributed outside of the POC's control."

• "No society in human history has confronted an enemy as omnipresent as the US corporate media. Yet there is no choice but to challenge their hegemony."

• The investigative reporters of the various cited websites should be encouraged to explore the possibilities of joining together to initiate a new nationwide radio and television networks. Ultimate aim of this new network should be to collect and convey the facts that every citizen must know in the interest of proper functioning of the democracy.

• Every media is very much interested in making money and hence they are actively competing against each other to get the best possible rating at all times. Excellent rating means more money through more media commercial advertisements.

• The media's first and foremost duty must be to serve the people by providing all the information that the people need to know for the proper functioning of the democracy.

• The media's real objective is to ensure that the corporate interests are protected and provided for at any cost and by any means. So, in their own subtle way the media continues to do every thing they can to keep the republicans at the helm, but not the democrats.

• The media wants the government to serve the interests of the greedy corporations but not the interests of the people who elect the government. This is the tragedy.

• The rich and the right wings control most of the USA networks. They know the best ways on how to fool the people while making money using the people.

• Please checkout the four suggestions cited above for a possible solution.

The Awesome Destructive Power
of the Corporate Power Media
by Glen Ford and Peter Gamble
www.dissidentvoice.org
February 2, 2004
First Published in The Black Commentator

Howard Dean has joined the list of victims of U.S. corporate media consolidation. Dean shares this distinction with <u>Dennis Kucinich</u> and the people of the formerly sovereign state of Iraq, among many others. Dean was stripped of <u>half</u> his popular support in the space of two weeks in January while John Kerry – tied in the polls with Carol Moseley-Braun at seven percent just <u>two months</u> earlier – rose like a genie from a bottle to become the overnight presidential frontrunner. Both candidates were shocked and disoriented by the dizzying turns of fortune, and for good reason. Neither Dean nor Kerry had done anything on their own that could have so dramatically altered the race. Corporate America decided that Dean must be savaged, and its media sector made it happen.

This commentary, however, is not about the <u>merits of Howard Dean</u>. If a mildly progressive, Internet-driven, young white middle class-centered, movement-like campaign such as Dean's -- flush with money derived from unconventional sources, backed by significant sections of labor, reinforced by big name endorsements and surging with upward momentum -- can be derailed in a matter of weeks at the whim of corporate media, then all of us are in deep trouble. The Dean beat-down should signal an intense reassessment of media's role in the American power structure. The African-American historical experience has much to offer in that regard, since the Civil Rights and Black Power Movements were born in a wrestling match with an essentially hostile corporate (white) media. However, there can be no meaningful discussion of the options available to progressive forces in the United States unless it is first recognized that the corporate media in the current era is the enemy, and must be treated that way.

It is no longer possible to view commercial news media as mere servants of the ruling rich -- they are full members of the presiding corporate pantheon. General media consolidation has created an integrated mass communications system that is both objectively and self-consciously at one with the Citibanks and ExxonMobils of the world. Media companies act in effective unison on matters of importance to the larger corporate class. For all politically useful purposes, the monopolization of US media is now complete, in that the corporate owners and managers of the dominant organs are interchangeable and indistinguishable, sharing a common mission and worldview. (That's the underlying reason why their "news" product is nearly identical.)

Monopolies do not require a solitary actor -- an ensemble acting in concert achieves the same results.

In the past year we have seen consciousness-shaking evidence of the corporate media's implacable hostility to any manifestation of resistance to the current order. Media rushed to embed themselves in the US war machine's Iraq invasion, and collaborated to actively suppress public awareness of a full-blown movement against the war. Hundreds of thousands of protestors were made to <u>disappear</u> in plain sight. Corporate media conspired -- which is what businessmen in boardrooms do as a matter of daily routine -- not only to shield the public from dissenting opinions (their usual assignment), but to drastically diminish, distort and even erase huge gatherings that were profoundly newsworthy by any rational standard. This is not mere bias, but the end result of the corporate decision making process. There is no line separating "news" producers from larger corporate structures, nor can media companies be neatly segregated from the oligarchic herd. Corporate media's ties to the Pirates in Washington are organic and nearly seamless. Their collusion seems almost telepathic, because they share the same class and worldview -- the most far reaching consequence of media consolidation.

The corporate media is a window on the dialogue among the rich. They are saying loudly and uniformly that even mild resistance to their rule will be treated as illegitimate and subjected to censorship and ridicule by their media organs. The scope of tolerable dissent has been narrowed, as reflected in the behavior of corporate media. The Dean beat-down is just the latest twist in the tightening of the screws.

The thoroughly Republican nature of corporate opinion molding mechanisms is evident in their treatment of Bill Clinton and Al Gore. The media giants subjected Clinton to the full fury of the Hard Right's campaign to destabilize his presidency, ultimately resulting in impeachment hearings. Al Gore, a sitting vice-president seeking the top job in 2000, was reduced to a caricature by the corporate press corps and punditry—the torture of a thousand daily cuts. Gore's cardboard image was the cumulative product of relentless corporate press commentary, disguised as reportage. Jay Leno and the other late night jokers feed off carrion that has already been slaughtered by corporate "news" media.

Clinton's Republican predecessors were not subjected to anything approaching such scrutiny and abuse. It is self-evident that George Bush, who should have been buried under a glacier of scandal and criminality within months of entering the White House, enjoys the full-time protection of the corporate press. Their institutional intention is to elect him again. Media apologists offer fictions about press vs. power, when in reality corporate media = corporate power, just as Bush = corporate power. The Democrats are not part of this equation.

Thus, the rich men's media descended on the Democratic Party primary process in order to mangle and denigrate it, while propping up the corporate champion in the White House. The *New York Times*, through its chief political reporter, Adam Nagourney, set the parameters of coverage by eliminating any *mention* of the three "bottom tier" candidates -- starting with his "analysis" of the May televised <u>debate</u> in South Carolina, a state in which Al Sharpton is a key player! Nagourney systematically erased Sharpton, Kucinich and Carol Moseley-Braun from his weekly coverage of the contest -- a professionally suicidal routine were it not consistent with the objectives of corporate management. The *Times* proudly sets the standard for national reporting, but its leadership was not necessary to ensure that the bottom tier would remain at the bottom. The organs of corporate speech all march to the same tune because there is not a dime's worth of difference between their owners.

Get rich or drop out

The corporate media's weapons are censorship and ridicule. Dennis Kucinich absorbed the full measure of both. However, TV "news" producers, mindful of viewer demographics, tried to avoid direct aggression against the characters of Moseley-Braun and Sharpton. ABC finally showed its true corporate colors at the New Hampshire debate in the person of *Nightline's* Ted Koppel. Imperiously addressing the bottom trio, <u>Koppel</u> said:
"You've [to Kucinich] got about $750,000 in the bank right now, and that's close to nothing when you're coming up against this kind of opposition. But let me finish the question. The question is, will there come a point when polls, money and then ultimately the actual votes that will take place here in places like New Hampshire, the caucuses in Iowa, will there come a point when we can expect one or more of the three of you to drop out? Or are you

in this as sort of a vanity candidacy?"

Kucinich, Sharpton and Moseley-Braun acquitted themselves well in the exchange. The real story here is that Koppel felt *empowered* to all but demand that the three most progressive candidates (and both Blacks) vacate the Democratic presidential arena. Koppel had fumed to the New York Times about the uppity intruders, the month before. The day after the debate, ABC withdrew its reporters from all three campaigns. (None of the other networks had even bothered to give full-time coverage to the bottom tier.)

Koppel's arrogance, so unbecoming to a journalist, is rooted in his actual status at ABC/Disney: he is a corporate executive who pretends to be a newsman on television. His professional history notwithstanding, Koppel and each of the high profile TV "news" personalities are millionaire executives who act as spokesmen for the corporate divisions of their parent companies. They interact with executives of other divisions, principally marketing -- the domain of sales and "impressions." Koppel is incapable of thinking in terms other than money and polls, an important marketing tool. He is proprietary about the political process because, as an esteemed executive in the ruling corporate class, he thinks he owns it.

Self-fulfilling prophesy

Howard Dean's brilliant use of the Internet allowed him to capitalize on anti-war sentiment while assembling a funding base independent of the usual corporate suspects. Dean's December surge took the corporate media by surprise, alarming the bosses and their friends in the White House. Like a Mormon Tabernacle Choir, the corporate media rose with one voice to question Dean's "electability." It is important to note that in mid-December, according to *Newsweek's* poll, Dean, Kerry and Clark were doing equally in a match-up with George Bush, at 40, 41, and 41 percent, respectively. There was no statistical basis to single out Dean as unelectable. Dean had just gotten the endorsement of Al Gore and two of the nation's most important unions, AFSCME and SEIU. No matter. The corporate media has the power of self-fulfilling prophesy, and they know it. Negative impressions rained down on Dean like a monsoon, and didn't let up even after the damage was done. Dean was tagged by the media as a loser to Bush well before he let out "The Scream" -- an innocuous, non-event, on the night of his Iowa defeat.

Dean understands what was done to him, although there's nothing much he can do about it. In an interview with *CNN*'s repugnant Wolf Blitzer, the candidate said: "You report the news and you create the news… You chose to play it ["The Scream"] 673 times."

It is clear from the numbers that Democratic voters, determined to be rid of George Bush, were afraid to support the "unelectable" Dean. Lots of them ran to Kerry, who had polled at only 7 percent nationally in November. Kerry had done and said nothing to affect this sea change. The irony here is that it is Bush who is so scary to Democratic voters that they backed away from Dean, whom the corporate media had pegged as a "scary" guy.
Chris Bowers offered a compelling analysis of the corporate media coup in the January 28 *Daily Kos*:

In order to reduce the increasing control of the Political Opinion Complex over our political process, we need to begin developing and strengthening institutions strong enough to counter its current influence. Specifically, we need to further develop networks where political information can be mass distributed outside of the POC's control. Not long ago, there were several such outside institutions. Unions and churches were a far more pervasive part of people's lives. Newspapers and periodicals were significantly more numerous and varied in their political outlook. Public television and radio had far larger audiences. Political parties and societies were either machines or at least overflowing with active members. All of these now weakened institutions once served as means to perform end-runs outside the control of the corporate media and the Political Opinion Complex. Engagement with the political process through means other than television was far greater. However, those institutions no longer serve as significant counter-weights to the strength of the Political Opinion Complex

African Americans faced a much more hostile establishment (white) press in the days of Jim Crow, local newspapers that often incited mob violence against Blacks and, on occasion, announced lynchings in advance. In the Fifties, Blacks employed informal and church networks and the Black press (where it existed) to create mass movements -- facts on the ground that could not be ignored. The Montgomery Bus Boycott and, later, mass marches and jail-ins in Birmingham drew the attention of the northern-based corporate media. More interested in recording the show than supporting the protestors, the media nevertheless served to fire up the spirit of Black America and hasten the demise of Jim Crow.

As the Sixties unfolded, mass incendiary activity presented the media and nation with additional facts -- burning cities are not easily ignored. The corporate press grudgingly integrated their staffs. Although Black newspapers went into steep decline, Black radio sprouted news departments that encouraged local organizers to tackle the tasks of a post-Civil Rights world. Thirty years later, media consolidation has had the same strangulating effects on Black radio as in the general media. Radio One, the largest Black-owned chain, recently entered into a <u>marketing agreement</u> with a subsidiary of Clear Channel, the 1200-station beast. Both chains abhor the very concept of local news.

There is no question that Blacks and progressives must establish alternative media outlets, and not just on the Internet. However, there is no substitute for <u>confronting the corporate media</u> head-on, through direct mass action and other, creative tactics. The rich men's voices must be de-legitimized in the eyes of the people, who already suspect that we are being systematically lied to and manipulated. African-Americans have an advantage in this regard, since they are used to being lied to and about.

No society in human history has confronted an enemy as omnipresent as the US corporate media. Yet there is no choice but to challenge their hegemony. The world can be changed, but only by changing the way others see their world.

Glen Ford and Peter Gamble are the editors of <u>The Black Commentator,</u> where this article first appeared.

Marriage and Family life

As we all know, our community and society consist of families. If we want to have a loving and caring community where people help each other and live happily and harmoniously, then we should have families that have this type of attitude and approach in their day-to-day lives. So, let us checkout what type of family do we have.

Are you one of those fortunate few who have a happily married family life? Yes? Lucky you!!! Let our God Almighty continue to bless you and your family for a sustained happiness all your lives. As you seem to be an example of how to lead a happy family life, let us not dwell any further on blessed people like you.

We all aim to have a happy married family life. Unfortunately, especially in the Western culture, 1 in 2 marriages end up in divorces. Why? What is it that we are doing wrong?

Prior to our marriage, whether it is an arranged marriage or a love marriage, we all have so much of aspirations and dreams to make the marriage a real great success. But, quite a few of us are not that fortunate to realize that dream and success.

In the case of arranged marriages, like how it normally used to be in the Eastern culture, the love between the man and the woman develops after the wedding. Understandably, it may sound strange for the people who are born and brought up in the Western culture. But, believe it or not, most of the arranged marriages surprisingly last longer than the love marriages. The main reason for this is basically the expectations, the way of thinking and the mental make up of the bride and groom as formed and developed by the social set up and the culture in which they grow up. Pre-marital sexual relationship was very rare during those days. As such, just after the marriage they start enjoying each other in every aspect of the married life together. It is a new thrilling experience and adventure. The lust dominates and the love develops slowly, steadily and strongly. Then, within a few years, there comes their offspring. Naturally as young new parents, they are devoted towards the welfare and upbringing of that offspring. Thus, now you have a new common bond that binds you both with a common objective. Except in some rare instances, invariably, in most of the cases the love and care for each other continues to grow forever. Besides, there is quite a lot of give and take in most cases. This is what I can think of as the real reasons for the success of the arranged marriages. I may be wrong, but that is all I know of.

Because of whatever I said herein about the success of a number of arranged marriages, please do not for a moment think that I am here to advocate for an arranged marriage. All I convey is my understanding of how and why most of the arranged marriages seem to last long.

Having said that, I also know of quite a number of arranged marriages that have already ended in divorces or are on the verge of collapse. The reason for this, in most cases, is the male domination. As long as the wife just obeys and does everything the husband wants everything goes okay. But, the trouble starts the moment the woman rightfully tries to exercise her independence and expresses her views as an individual. When this happens, the man of the house turns like a beast from the jungle. To the best of my knowledge, the man is the main culprit for the failure of an arranged marriage. His attitude is just to take and take, but not to give and take. He thinks that he is just "be all and end all." He has no regard or respect for his partner's views or likes and dislikes. To cut the story short, it is the male chauvinism that ruins the marriages in most of these cases.

One main common factor in any relationship, whether it is a marriage or just a friendship, is the compatibility between the persons concerned. If you are courting your partner with a view to eventually getting married, then this is the right period to checkout how compatible you two are. Of course, no two persons will have exactly similar likes and dislikes. The compatibility between you two will very rarely be exceptionally good or excellent. But, if it is pretty good, then the chances of having a successful marriage will also be pretty good. If the compatibility is reasonably good and you two are really in love, but not being or living together just for lust, then there is a chance of working out on those minor differences to ensure a successful marriage. But, if the compatibility is very little, then there is no point in wasting your time any further hoping that he or she will change eventually to ensure a successful marriage. I'm afraid, it won't happen as this is the reality. A person's character and behaviour can only be slightly modified, but definitely cannot be changed considerably. If you are facing these unfortunate circumstances, then please call it off for good and look elsewhere for your compatible partner. If you are in love or infatuated with your partner, but your partner is not reciprocating or responding positively in tune with your expectations, please realize the fact that you cannot force a person to love or care for you. This has to come from within spontaneously. I'm sure that you will find the right person when you make a careful and considered search for that person. Someone is there waiting for you with similar expectations and doing a similar search.

The root cause of most of our social problems is because of broken or unstable families. Most of the children from single parent families or from families where the parents bicker most of the time tend to have unsecured feelings about their immediate and future lives. As a result, they don't do well with their studies, but instead tend to get into all types of undesirable mischief and vandalism. To be fair, it is not their fault.

As briefed before in the "Violence" chapter, we, the parents, should take full responsibility in this context since, whether it is deliberate or not, we drove them to pursue that path. We must remember the fact that our kids are like wet clay. We can shape the wet clay to look like an angel or like a monster. It is we who brought them into existence. If we are not mentally matured enough to bring them up properly teaching them the virtues and values of good life in a society followed by sustained real monitoring of their day-to-activities and behaviour, then we should not have had the children. We may not like to accept this basic fact. No useful purpose will be served in trying to find excuses in this respect. If your child turned out to be a big bully terrorizing other kids, yes, it is your fault. If your kids deal drugs, yes, it is your fault. We can go on and on like this on this issue.

So, let us do a self-assessment on what type of parent we are and see how best we can do concerning corrective course of action, if need be.

Let us consider the case of a single parent family. If you happen to be one of those unfortunate few, we all know that it is extremely difficult for you to concentrate on your work that you do for living while you try to be both mother and father for your children and hopefully pursue some personal physical and emotional happiness for yourself. But, sadly, for some reason or other you are forced to cope up with the situation as best you can. This demands a lot on your personal character, patience and perseverance to do the right things at the right time.

Again, when the kids go through peer pressure, especially during the transition period from childhood to adulthood, the problem gets more cumulative. Under these circumstances, it is essential that you keep your kids fully aware of everything you do for them. This will make them realize what a great parent you are to sacrifice your own personal life in their interest and as such they too in turn will try to help you in every possible way they can to make your life a bit easy to manage.

It is true, being just a normal human being, there may be occasions when you may loose your cool and take out your pent up pressure on your kids. Please try to avoid doing this and instead get your kids emotionally involved with everything you do. Encourage them to actively participate in arts, music and sports. This will keep them mentally fully occupied and will help them to get into some sort of self-induced discipline. Whenever and wherever possible, spend quality time with your kids participating in their school, sport and cultural activities. Besides being the parent, try and be their buddy as well so that your kids can feel free to convey their feelings and frustrations with you all the time without any reservation or hesitation. Communicate with them all the time. Share your feelings and problems with them. Make them realize that you are there for them and they are there for you. In short, make them realize that you both sink or sail together as one team. Consistently and constantly shower them with your love and care. Once they are aware of this fact, then nothing can stop them from reciprocating to you in a positive way. **Love is the most powerful binding force between people.**

Don't impose your views on them. Encourage them to be creative. Find out what their expectations, aspirations and dreams about their life in general and future in particular are. Encourage them and help them to pursue their dreams, if you consider that it is in the right direction. But, if it is not in line with your way of thinking or expectations, then advise your kids as to why you think that it may not be in their best interest. Please note that you should try and advise, but should not insist and impose. This type of forcing them to go against what they want to do, will only lead to unpleasant friction and eventual end to the loving relationship between you two.

I am sure, there will be some organisations around you where you can get some professional advice from people who are trained to teach various "DOs" and "DON'Ts" for your particular case. Please try and make the best use of this type of services. Patience, perseverance and sincere prayer to maintain your sanity only seem to be the best solution for your situation. Let God bless you with the best of the bests to enable you to find some happiness and bring up your kids as good caring and sharing citizens.

Now, let us consider the case of broken or unstable family where parents still live together. Over the years, the couples may find themselves to be incompatible to co-exist. But, some of these marriages still seem to last long, irrespective of whether they are happy together or not. In many cases, this is mainly because of the cultural and social up bringing. But, here the problem is that invariably the male dominates and the woman obeys, irrespective of what her feelings and views are. This is mainly because of pressure from the society, especially in the Eastern culture, and in the interests of the welfare of the children. The moment the woman rightfully tries to assert her views, the male who thinks that he is God Almighty tries to put her down. It is wrong. She has every right as a human being and as a partner-in-life to express and enforce her views especially when those views are right and justifiable. Whether it is a love marriage or arranged marriage, continued and sustained love and care, give and share, should be the guiding principles for a successful, happy married life. Come what may, ***male chauvinism must stop,*** if you are really serious about a happy married life.

Having said that, now let us look at the other side of the coin also. I am sure, we have come across quite a number of cases where the woman dominates and the man, in the interest of peace at home, says "yes" to everything without any objection. In this context, let me just brief two jokes that I happen to read somewhere.

The first one goes like this. On one Sunday, a priest asked the men who attended the church service as follows: "All those men who are like henpecks, please raise your hand." Almost all, except for just two, raised their hands.

The priest thought that perhaps those two who did not raise their hands may not know the meaning of 'henpeck.' So, he looked at one of those two men and asked whether he understood what 'henpeck' means. That man said, "Of course, I do. I did not raise my hand because my wife told me not to."

The second joke goes like this. A bunch of couples got together for a gossip evening. You know how gossip goes around, especially when the gossip victim is not around. While they were chatting, one woman said, "You know, Angela is always bossy and would not let her husband decide and do what he wants. I am not at all like that. My Mike makes all the decisions on major issues like nuclear disarmament, world peace, war on terror, etc. But, I just decide on what every one in my family should do. That is all."

This type of domination from either side is not conducive for a happy married life. Marriage is a sacred union where the man and the woman join together as partners-in-life to share every aspect of their life together. It is an equal partnership, but definitely not the master and slave relationship. It is possible, invariably because in most cases the man is a bit older than the woman and as a result has some added experience in life, the man may have a better practical approach to attend to the day-to-day problems. But, the main thing here is, the man must convince his wife in a loving and caring way explaining why he thinks it is better to do the way he suggests. At the same time, he must listen to her views also with all sincerity. When it comes to the matters related to the family, mothers are more balanced than men. So, consider carefully her views also. At the end, make a collective decision in the interest of the family as a whole. Never ever try to impose your views on each other. Communicate, consult, and consider each other's views and then arrive at a collective decision. If things happen to go wrong after this collective decision, then you won't be at each other's throat since it is your joint decision.

We are on our toes all the time chasing money. It is true, money is very important. But, we forget the fact that it is not everything. Let me add herein what I read recently somewhere:

- Money can buy a house, but not home.
- Money can buy a bed, but not sleep.
- Money can buy a clock, but not time.

- Money can buy a book, but not knowledge.
- Money can buy position, but not respect.
- Money can buy sex, but not love.
- Money can buy medicine, but not health.
- Money can buy blood, but not life.

One of you may be a worrying type trying to find answers for all type of "what if" questions. This is one of the most destructive forces in a married life. I am aware that this person is not worrying deliberately. It is like some form of illness with that person. People are different. However, this worrying person must realize that this type of constant worrying will only contribute towards high blood pressure, but not towards the happiness in life. Of course, we all must have "Plan A," "Plan B," etc. But, we must not get boggled down to the details of imagining and worry about the worse all the time.

We all have quite a bit of our "needs" and "wants." Whenever we tend to worry thinking that I am not able to get this and that, please remember to be happy and grateful to our God Almighty for what we are blessed with while, at the same time, try your best to work hard to get what you are aiming for. We must try and be careful in whatever we do. At the same time, we must also realize that the life is short and we don't know what is in store for us the next minute. As such, enjoy your life to the best you can while trying to be careful in everything you do. Do the best you can and leave the rest to God since whatever will be will be.

Please read Dale Carnegie's books like *How to Stop Worrying and Start Living* that shows the practical way to overcome fears and anxieties in our day-to-day lives and *How to Win Friends and Influence People* that shows how to effectively get along with every one in our lives. These two books are excellent practical guides which when really put into practice will lead to a real happy life. There is no point in just reading. We must really practice the recommendations made therein. However, if your constant worrying habit happens to be something related to your genetics, then obviously you need to seek medical help. Hope it is not.

Another mistake we do in our life is this: Most of us worry, thinking that what will others say about whatever we are doing. Don't forget, we can't

PERUMAL KRISHNAN

live and lead our life to please others. You decide on whatever is the best in the interest of your family and get on with that. Just ignore what others may gossip about what you are doing. Irrespective of whatever you may do, good or bad, others will continue to find something or other to gossip about. This is because they have nothing better to do than to gossip. The one who gossips a lot is just an example of another form of evil in every society. None and nothing can stop them from gossiping about you. Whether you like it or not, that is how the human nature is. So, just stop worrying about gossips and carry on with whatever is good for your family. If you continue to worry about doing things just to please the gossipmongers, then you will ruin your happiness and that of your family. Stop it for good right now, if you want happiness in your life.

We need to sincerely try and attend to the physical and emotional needs of each other at all times. We are fully aware that cheating on your partner is wrong and is one of the major reasons for unhappiness in the family and breakdown of the marriages. As such, it is needless to emphasize that it must be avoided. But, if you ever happen to cheat on your partner, then for a moment please ask your conscience how you would feel if your partner did this to you. Besides, if you do it, then you should not blame your partner if he or she cheats on you. You are no better than your partner in this respect and as such have no right to question your partner. At the same time, you must realize that your children will have no respect or regard for the cheating person.

In this context, let me touch upon Mr. Clinton's episode. Of course, if he really did have illicit intimate affairs with other women, it is wrong. But, this is something the Clintons should sort out between themselves. It is none of my or anybody else's damn business in this respect. Definitely it is not that of the republicans' business to waste so much of taxpayers' money and legislative time. All those republicans who were hell bent on in this respect proved themselves to be real disgrace to our democracy. I am disappointed with Mr. Clinton as well. He is so smart and shrewd in everything he did for the welfare of the ordinary people. But, at the same time, how can he be that stupid to get into this real mess? He should know that living in the White House is like living in a glasshouse.

We can think of just two occasions when a couple can mutually enjoy themselves at the same time. One is when you are relaxing yourselves on a vacation at a place where both of you wanted to be. The other one is an obvious one that is an essential part of any married life.

Apart from that, we must realize the fact that each and every one of us is an individual and no two persons do have exactly similar likes and dislikes. As such, there is bound to be numerous occasions when what one does may not be what other would like. But, if the other person derives real happiness in doing whatever that may be, provided it does not hurt your family physically or emotionally or financially, then why don't you please let your partner enjoy? For example, you may be a sporty person and your partner may be a couch potato. In this case, encourage your partner to be active explaining all the good things that it will lead to. But, do not, repeat do not, constantly nag him or her on this count. Nagging is the last thing you must do, if you want to have a happy married life. But, if you are addicted to frequent shopping, spending a lot of money that you don't have, then you have a real problem and you need to get real and live within your means. Don't get carried away by the sales gimmicks. Buy things if, and only if, you need them and have place to keep them. I know of a number of friends who buy things simply because they are on sale, even though they don't need them and have no place to keep them. This type of addiction will ruin your family.

We can identify endless number of scenarios like this in this context. But, the main thing to note is never to nag and never to impose your views on to others. The motto should be "live and let live." Cherish all the good values and virtues of your partner instead of just picking on the partner's weakness all the time. Remember, marriage is a matter of give and take, but definitely not give, give or take, take all the time. Another point to note is this. Respecting each other is equally important like loving each other.

Of late, there has been a lot of uproar on gay people living together and wanting to get married. Personally, I believe that God created men and women to live together and mate each other to produce our future generations. But, in quite a few cases some people seem to have sexual orientation to the same sex partner. Honestly, I don't know what it is due to. But, here the point is this. What they do behind the closed doors to enjoy themselves is their business as long as they don't hurt others. God created us all. For some reason or other, some prefer to have sexual relationship with same sex partner.

Okay, let them enjoy themselves. Why should it bother you? They love each other, care about each other and want to live together as gay couple. Who are we to judge what they do or how they live? Just leave them alone. If they want to get married, for whatever reason it may be, give them your blessings. Please, don't give me all that moral or religious rubbish. They should not be treated as outcasts simply because they want to live and enjoy each other as gay couple. What is wrong with all those gays that excelled extremely well in the movie and tennis world, just to name a few? What harm did they do to others? NOTHING. They just minded their own business and so should you and me. Stop being the hypocrites of the 1st order.

Don't forget what you, the hypocrites, did in the past.

You pretended to preach and practice all the moral values by regularly attending the church, while at the same you were actively engaged in selling black people as slaves. Don't you think that your behaviour then was despicable?

You proclaimed that "all men are created equal." But, wouldn't give equal voting rights to all the black citizens to vote. By the way, you say "all men are created equal," what happened to the women? Don't they deserve recognition, respect, equal pay, etc? What is their role in the society? Are they just for pleasing you in the bed? You hypocrites make me sick.

The recent recommendation by Mr. Bush in favour of the amendment to the Constitution is nothing but another example of his numerous dumb decisions. There are quite a number of other pressing issues related to the democracy and safety of the citizens that need amendments to the constitution. As for me, just to name a few, we must seriously consider immediate amendments to the Constitution in respect of the following:

• The President of the USA must be decided by the popular votes, but not by electoral votes.
• All the nominations and appointments for the posts that are NOT related or relevant to the official administrations of the heads like President/ Governor/Mayor, etc. must be outside the control of the politicians. This includes all arenas where political influence should not exist. Please never ever forget the episode related to the real injustice done to the democracy

by the Supreme Court Justices when they selected Mr. Bush as the President in 2000.
• The concept of "right to bear arms" should be scrapped from the Constitution for good.

The parents have a major and main role to play on our children's upbringing. Almost in all cases, the kids look up to their parents as their role models. If you are good, then your kids will turn out to be good. If you are loving and caring type, then your kids will become like that too.

So, What sort of role model are you to your kids? Let us have a brief look at this.

Of course, you love and care for your kids dearly. Do you express your love in every conceivable way so that your kids realize that they are loved and cared for? Kids, especially in the early stage, invariably tend to copy what the elders do. So, when they are convinced that they are loved dearly, they will try to do the same to others, starting with their toys.

If you are a violent type of person, throwing things, swearing, shouting and screaming at others, then the kids get really scared. In turn, they take out their fear and frustration on others, starting with their toys again.

Let us do a self-assessment on our attitude and behavior in our normal day-to-day routine.

Say, you normally get up very early in the morning to get ready to go to work. The other family members are still in bed. Do you make a sincere effort to make your moves gently and softly so that you do not disturb others who are still trying to sleep? Or, you just don't care, but bang the doors and play the radio or TV loudly. Please remember, the kids will never ever forget this type of inconsiderate, arrogant and unpleasant behaviour. No wonder, they may turn out to be like you.

Say, you are driving your car to get to work. Do you maintain a safe driving distance between your car and the car in front? Do you eat and drink while you drive? Do you smoke while you drive? Do you use your hand held mobile phone while you drive? Do you use the indicators? Don't you realize that it will take just a second to get involved in an accident? You may be a careful driver. But, how about the other drivers? Won't you need your both hands free in the event of other erratic driver suddenly coming in your way? Don't you think, it is sensible and even may be life saving to pull up the car somewhere in a safe place and then eat, drink, smoke and use the phone? Do you play the music in your car too loud to the extent that other drivers on the road can listen to your music? Don't you think that it is very inconsiderate of you to do that? You decide. When children watch elders with these bad driving habits, they just copy it.

Okay, you are at work now. How sincere, conscientious, dedicated and devoted are you to your assigned responsibilities in return for the pay you get? If you are like this, besides the possible promotion and more pay, your children will feel so proud of you and follow your path in their life as well.

Okay, all of you, the family members, got back home after the day's routine and schedule at work and school. Now, it is the time for the family to join together to help each other and find out how the day went by with everyone's activities. Do you openly communicate and share with each other all the good and bad that happened on that day? This type of communication is very important to keep the binding between all of you in tact. Listen to what each other has to say. Congratulate and convey any constructive criticism as appropriate to each other.

Now it is time to relax a bit by watching some television programs. What sorts of programs or movies do you all watch? Is it the violent and vulgar type where the program is full of foul language and obscene scenes? Or, is it the type of program that is inspirational and thought provoking? The 2nd choice will help to motivate the children to move in the positive direction to become caring and sharing citizens.

After you finish the shopping, do you make it a point to return the cart to the space allocated for it or you just leave it anywhere in the parking lot? Just imagine, say, you have a beautiful BMW that you parked in the parking lot. When you get back to the car after shopping, how will you feel if a shopping cart rolled around and hit your BMW making a big dent in your expensive car? Don't say that it is very rare. I have seen this happening on numerous occasions during windy days. Don't you think that it is just common sense and courtesy expected out of any decent human being to leave the cart back where it should be left? Please remember that our children do exactly what we do.

Besides, just for ready reference, let me copy the relevant section of "Violence" chapter that is appropriate here.

We can do the following hopefully to make them as good citizens:

• Try and spend as much of time as possible with your child.
• Be not only a parent but also a real good friend so that the child feels comfortable to confide anything and everything that he/she wants to share with.
• Help with the school homework, but don't do it for them.
• Constantly communicate with your child.
• Don't give them or encourage them to watch violent video games.
• Watch with them good inspiring movies like *Guess who is coming for dinner*, but definitely not the violent and vulgar movies like *Pulp Fiction*.
• If you are interested in watching any of the "R" rated movies or documentaries, then you do so when they are not around you.
• Besides the school background, children pick up foul languages from the movies. Since they are very susceptible for anything at that age, they think it is "cool" to talk and behave like those characters in the movies.
• Remember the saying, "tell me about your friends, then I will tell you about you." So, keep an eye on the type of friends your child has and move with.
• Encourage them to read a lot of biographies and autobiographies of legends like Mahatma Gandhi, Dr. Martin Luther King, Nelson Mandela, etc. etc., just to name a few that I know of.
• Encourage them to read a lot of inspiring books that will give them good guiding principles for a bright and better future.
• Encourage them to read Dale Carnegie's books like *How to Stop Worrying and Start Living* that shows the practical way to overcome fears and anxieties in our day-to-day lives and *How to Win Friends and Influence People* that shows how to effectively get along with every one in our lives. These two books are excellent practical guides which when really put into practice will lead to a real happy good life.

- Encourage them to get interested in games like basketball, soccer, etc. If you can afford, also encourage them to participate in tennis, golf, etc.
- Encourage them to get interested in arts, music, dancing etc.
- Keep them fully active and occupied both mentally and physically at all times.
- Be in close contact with your child's teacher to find out how the child is behaving and performing in the school. A child's character is moulded based on how good you and the teacher work towards it.
- Encourage the child to be creative and find out what his/her real interests and aspirations are. Check them out and encourage them to pursue them, if they are towards his/her better future.
- Make them realize the danger involved in using alcohol, drugs, cigarettes, etc.
- Motivate and encourage the children to go to the places of worship. But, never ever let the children believe in violence as the means to get whatever they may want. Remember what is happening in the Middle East, Northern Island, India and Pakistan. Violence should never be a part of your religious faith.

Bringing up a child as a good citizen is not an easy task. It is never ending. Good things don't just happen. We have to work really hard to get them.

Points for *Something to Think About*:

- If we want a loving and caring community where people help each other and live happily and harmoniously together, then we need families that have this type of attitude and approach in their day-to-day lives.
- In arranged marriages, the love between the couples develops after the wedding. Most of the arranged marriages surprisingly last longer than the love marriages. The reason for this is basically the expectations, the way of thinking and the mental make up of the bride and groom as formed and developed by the social set up and the culture in which they grow up.
- In most of those cases where the arranged marriages fail or failed, the main reason is the male chauvinism. The man fails to regard and respect

the views of his wife, but in turn behaves like the master and commander of the marriage. The trouble starts the moment the wife does not obey his wishes.

• The success or failure of a marriage depends on the compatibility between the couples.

• If the compatibility is reasonably good and the couples are really in love, but not being or living together just for lust, there is a chance to work out the minor differences to make the marriage a success.

• A person's character and behaviour can only be modified slightly, but definitely cannot be changed considerably.

• You cannot force a person to love or care for you since this has to come from within spontaneously.

• The root cause of most of our social problems is the broken or unstable families since the children from these families tend to have unsecured feelings about their immediate and future lives.

• If the couples are not mentally matured enough to bring up the children properly teaching them all the virtues and values of good life in a society, followed by sustained monitoring of their day-to-day activities and behaviour, then the couples should not have had the children. They are unfit parents.

• The couples should shower their kids with all the love and care and ensure that the kids realize that.

• Encourage the kids to actively participate in arts, music and sports. This will keep them mentally occupied and will help them to have some sort of self-induced discipline. Whenever and wherever possible, spend quality time with your kids by participating in their school, sport and cultural activities. Besides, try and be their buddy so that they feel free to convey their feelings and frustrations with you always without any reservation or hesitation. Communicate with them constantly. Share your feelings and problems with them. Make them realize that you are there for them, and they are there for you.

• Love is the most powerful binding force between the peoples in the world.

• Don't impose your views on your kids. Help and encourage them to be creative. Find out their expectations, aspirations and dreams about their life in general and future in particular are. Encourage them and help them to pursue their dreams, if you consider that it is in the right direction. But, if it is not as per your way of thinking or expectations, then advice your kids as to why you think that it may not be in their best interest. Please advise, but do not insist or impose your views. Forcing them to do against what they want to do will only lead to unpleasant friction and eventual end to the loving relationship between you two.

• Continued and sustained love and care along with give and share and respect for each other should be the guiding principle for a successful happy married life. No male or female domination should ever be there for a happy married life.

• Marriage is a sacred union where the man and the woman join together as partners-in-life to share every aspect of their life together. It is an equal partnership, but definitely not the master and slave relationship.

• Never ever try to impose your views on each other. Communicate, consult and consider each other's views and then arrive at a joint collective decision.

• Constant worrying habit is the most destructive force in a marriage.

• Life is short and we don't know what is in store for us the next minute. So, enjoy your life to the best you can while trying to be careful in everything you do. Do the best you can and leave the rest to God since whatever will be will be.

• Stop worrying about what others will say about what you do. You can't live and lead your life to please others. Whatever you may do, good or bad, others will always find something or other to gossip about. There is nothing you can do to stop them doing so, except to concentrate on your life and the way you want to lead it.

• Cheating on your partner is the foremost reason for unhappiness in the family and breakdown of the marriages.

• Everyone is an individual by himself/herself and no two persons have exactly similar likes and dislikes.

• Nagging is the last thing you do, if you want to have a happy married life.

• "Never to nag," "never to impose your views" and "live and let live" should be the guiding principles for a successful marriage. Cherish all the virtues of your partner. Don't pick on partner's weakness. Marriage is a matter of give and take, but definitely not give, give or take, take all the time. Respecting each other is as important as loving each other.

• What consenting adults do behind the closed doors to enjoy each other is their business as long as they don't hurt others.

• Whatever we may think of the gay couples, we have no right to tell them how they should lead their life. They love each other, care about each other and want to live together. They don't do any harm to others. Just leave them alone. If they want to get married, give them your blessings. They just mind their own business and so should we.

• The kids look up to their parents as their role models. If you are good, then your kids will turn out to be good. If you are loving and caring type, then your kids will become like that too. The children, especially in the early stage, invariably tend to copy what we, the elders, do.

Race and Religion

Any discrimination based on the individual's race or religion is not only illegal, but above all it is immoral. We have heard so many sad stories related to the racial discriminations over the years. Whether we like to admit or not, still the discrimination exists though not to the same extent as it did before. There are some improvements in race relations. We had to go through a lot of long struggles to get where we are now. But, still we have a long way to go, unfortunately. We are not quite there yet when it comes to equal opportunity in higher education and good employment for the minorities.

Let whatever be the race we are supposed to belong to, still we are all God's children since we are God's creation. We may have variations as regards to our features, characters, and skin colours. But, still each and every one of us is God's child. So, as for me, in the eyes of our Almighty we all belong to just one race viz. human race. Period. I may be wrong. But, my guess is, all this classification of white race, black race, etc. is the work of some evil white men in the distant past to exploit the people of other colour to take care of the white people's evil vested interests.

Irrespective of our skin colours, we all know that our blood has always been red, but not white, or black, or brown, or yellow. Basically, like any other human being, we all have the same desire to be loved, recognized, and respected by others. We all have same or similar type of selfishness and greed. Even within our own family, each of us is different by colour, feature and behaviour. Again, we may not agree on everything that each of us does. We may argue a lot, let whatever be the reason for it; but, do we fight and kill each other simply because of this difference? NO. We agree to disagree and learn to live together as one family. For heaven sake, why can't we please extend this sane and sensible approach beyond our own family to include everyone living in our community, country and other countries as well?

I believe that good and bad exist in every race, community and country.

These attributes are not confined to any one particular race, or group of people. Mahatma Gandhi and the killer Nathuram Godse were both from the same country and same religion. The most popular Michael Jordan and the most controversial Dennis Rodman are both from the same race and played for the same team. Both Carter and Bush are American White Presidents, Carter caring for the poor and Bush caring for the rich. In short, we find good and bad everywhere irrespective of the race, religion, community and country.

So, whenever anything bad happens, like robbery or rape or shooting or murder, the present attitude of the media stereotyping "the suspect is a black" and "the suspect is a Hispanic," etc. must stop once and for all. I haven't heard the media ever saying that "the suspect is a white." Don't we find a lot of white thugs terrorizing the community? Are these brutal atrocities are arising from non-whites only? Why just pick on, and brand the blacks or Hispanics only, whenever any of the cited violence occurs? Most of these thugs, including the white thugs, are from the poor and broken families. This is not an excuse, but this is one of the major contributing factors. The media must do everything it can to promote racial harmony to realize Dr. King's dreams instead of spreading hatred towards the non-whites. The media is the main culprit in this respect.

Do you remember the most powerful speech, viz. "I Have A Dream" that was delivered on August 28, 1963 by Dr. Martin Luther King?

Please check out on *http://www.mecca.org/~crights/dream.html*.

Whenever people talk about racial hatred and discrimination, normal tendency is to think that it is the whites that do the discrimination to other races, blacks in particular. It was, and it is true, but only partly though. I know of a lot of blacks and Asians who discriminate and hate others exactly like how the whites do. Even though it is fully understandable because of all the atrocities that whites inflicted on other races over the years, it is equally wrong and immoral to hate whites as well. It is time to move on to ensure racial harmony.

Like how Dr. King said, "Let us not seek to satisfy our thirst for freedom by drinking from the cup of bitterness and hatred." We must look at our future with a positive outlook and work towards racial harmony so that we realize the dreams of Dr. Martin Luther King. Each and every one of us must do all we can to **"live in a nation where they will not be judged by the colour of their skin but by the content of their character." "And if America is to be a great nation, this must come true."**

I don't know, when or if that will ever happen. But, we must strive hard **"to speed up that day when all of God's children, black men and white men, Jews and Gentiles, Protestants and Catholics, will be able to join hands and sing in the words of the old Negro spiritual 'Free at last! Free at last! Thank God Almighty, we are free at last.'"**

As mentioned before, there have been some improvements. Some ethnic minorities have worked really hard to elevate the level of their status to a better state, as compared to the status and conditions their parents or they would have had in the past. It is encouraging. Even though Collin Powell and Dr. Rice are part of the evil Bush Administration that caused so much of chaos to this great nation, I have my utmost admiration and respect for their accomplishments. Just imagine, the hardships that they would have gone through to get where they are now. It would not have been easy at all. But, they had their potential, determination, and hard work to reach their American dreams. We can also identify a number of other celebrities who are rich and famous like Oprah Winfrey, Magic Johnson, Tiger Woods, Denzel Washington, etc., etc., just to name a few. We see some exceptional ethnic minorities excelling themselves in the sports, music and movie entertainment fields. I feel so happy when I see the people of all races, like those who play basketball, football, etc., hugging each other and congratulating each other in the court and fields. This is what Dr. King was dreaming about. Even some of the racially biased white spectators, who can't digest the idea of some of these black players making millions, congratulate those black players when they are part of their favorite teams. This is great. Even though I hate the violence in most of the sports like American football, professional wrestling, boxing, ice hockey, etc., I am so happy that the sports proved as an area where mixed races can mingle nicely together as one unit working towards the same purpose. It should not stop just there in the sport arena. This type of racial harmony should extend everywhere in every walk of life. Even though the ideals and aspirations of the "Affirmative Action" may not be welcomed by considerable number of the white population, this Affirmative Action must be strengthened and reinforced in the fields of education and employment for some more time, until such time where ethnic minorities can equip themselves with equal good education and employment opportunities. There is no need for any Affirmative Action in the sports or music or movie entertainment fields. The minorities have proved and excelled themselves in spite of all the hardships that they had to go through towards their success. These people must be congratulated for their achievements and success. It is not too long ago when the sports in England and America, like cricket, soccer, tennis, golf etc. were classified as exclusively elite white people's sports. I am glad that those days have gone for good now. However, I feel that still there needs to be some more unbiased mental maturity in respect toward the Oscar Academy Awards. We are getting there slowly and steadily, but not quite there yet. Hope it won't be too long to get there.

Mr. Bush has never been enthusiastic to uplift the welfare of the poor and minorities. So, as expected, he was opposed to the principles and functioning of the Affirmative Action.

As per, *http://www.affirmativeaction.org/UofM-Cases-2003.html,*
"Recently, Mr. Bush issued a statement to the U.S. Supreme Court that strongly opposes the University of Michigan admissions process as nothing more than an illegal quota system. Rather than let the Court hear the arguments when they are presented a few months from now, Mr. Bush has weighed in on the debate in order to influence the decisions of the Justices."

As per, *http://www.bamn.com/wdc/,*
"An unprecedented, public divide between President Bush and Secretary of State Colin Powell over the University of Michigan affirmative action policies illustrates the peculiar importance of these cases."

As per, *http://www.now.org/nnt/spring-2003/viewpoint.html,*
"There has always been affirmative action in higher education — but for many years it operated to exclude, rather than include, women and people of color. Consider one example: There is little doubt that George W. Bush's grades were lower than those of hundreds of students who were rejected by Yale University the same year Bush was welcomed there.

Yes, George W. Bush was a beneficiary of one kind of affirmative action— the kind that favored the sons of overwhelmingly white and well-to-do Yale graduates. Yet there was no White House denunciation of the "extra points" universities, including Michigan, give to children of donors or alums—only a condemnation of efforts to offset those preferences (which go mostly to white students) by also considering race and ethnic background.

Conservatives have called the Michigan plan everything but un-American, and that's probably coming soon. But what of college campuses, law schools and graduate schools, with nary a black or brown face to be seen? That's what I call un-American.

Last December, Sen. Trent Lott, that born-again civil rights supporter, said, "I'm for affirmative action," in an interview with Black Entertainment Television. But where is he now? Where is Senate Majority Leader Bill Frist? Where are the conservatives who talk about opportunity but only offer excuses? In "Letters from a Birmingham Jail," Dr. Martin Luther King, Jr. said that perhaps the Ku Klux Klan and the White Citizens Council were not the greatest enemies of progress—instead he cautioned about "the white moderate" who says "I agree with you in the goal you seek, but I cannot agree with your methods. . ." Those words ring just as true 40 years later."

As for, "Affirmative Action in the Broadcasting Industry," please checkout *http://www.nowfoundation.org/issues/communications/tv/affirmative.html*, "Opponents of affirmative action are pressuring the FCC to eliminate all affirmative action outreach and recruitment directives. The FCC will likely issue new affirmative action rules, and our opponents will likely challenge them in court. Appointment of FCC Commissioners is by the President, however confirmation and the budget of the FCC is controlled by Congress. In the long term, supporters of affirmative action must put policymakers in each branch of government who support affirmative action."

Please note, I am not advocating Affirmative Action forever. As briefed before, this Affirmative Action is needed in the fields of education and employment **for some more time** until such time the minorities group also get good education and employment. That is all. There is no need for it once the right remedial actions for the injustice inflicted on those minorities have taken positive effect.

I have a request for all those successful celebrities from ethnic minority group. Through your extra-ordinary talent, tenacity and God's blessings you were able to elevate yourself to fame and finance of a reasonably good level. You deserve every appreciation since you earned every bit of it. But, at the same time, please also remember that still there are millions of under-privileged kids in your own respective minority group who get into all types of unwanted situations, such as dealing drugs, being a gang member, engaging themselves in robbery, rape, shooting, etc., purely because of poverty, lack of good education and guidance.

This is where I request your attention. **ALL** the celebrities like Oprah, Magic, Tiger, Denzel, etc., etc. may please co-ordinate and unite together for a common noble purpose of uplifting these unfortunate children. You all may jointly set up an establishment whose primary goal is to define, design and do everything that is needed to uplift the spirits of these unfortunate kids so that they think of you as their role models and become better motivated, talented, educated and well accomplished in whatever walk of life they wish to pursue. In my opinion, this is the best way for you to say a big THANKS to our God for the blessings that were bestowed upon you. Please consider this request seriously.

Please remember, once you extend your helping hands to these kids who worship you as their role models, there is nothing to stop them from reaching their American dreams. They will never ever forget you for your contribution in this context. You will be like their real living angels whom they can see physically in person. I sincerely beg and pray to you, the celebrities, to do this for our future generations. Please share a portion of your well-earned fortune to invest on the future of these unfortunate kids. We never know, one of these kids whom you help to grow up to be a real caring citizen may end up as a real caring President, unlike Mr. Bush. Hope and pray that you guys will consider my humble request seriously and take some positive action accordingly. Thanks.

Now, let us talk about religion. For most of us the religion has been a real dominant factor to give us the guiding principles to lead our lives. Let me state, at the outset, the fact that I don't know and don't want to know the preaching of any religion. I am sure that preachers of every religion will say so many things claiming how good it is, so on and so forth. All I am interested in is in witnessing how it is being practised, not preached, in our day-to-day real life. Because, according to me, that is what really matters.

What has been going on in Northern Ireland between the Protestants and Catholics? They have been hunting and killing each other by the name of the religion making a mockery of their faiths and beliefs. The Irish people have same culture and aspirations. I would like to see the religious preachers helping the people to help each other and to enable them to live happily and harmoniously together. But, we have been witnessing repeated violence and killings only over the years. This is because the extremists on either side use the religion as an excuse to get their personal and political agenda. The ordinary people are being used as the pawns by these extremists in their political game of chess for this purpose.

What has been going on between India and Pakistan, and inside India itself between Hindus and Muslims? Again, here also they have been hunting and killing each other by the name of religion. We find an almost similar story in this scenario also. The extremists impose their views and philosophies on others. The people from both India and Pakistan have a similar culture, food habits, way of living, etc. For heaven sake, both India and Pakistan were just one country until 1947 when British split the country into two before their departure for good from India. Instead of the preachers doing every thing possible to unify the people so that they live happily together as one community, these extremists instigate and induce violence between these two sets of believers.

What has been going on in the Middle East, one sect of Muslims killing the other sect of Muslims in the name of religion? Here also, we find almost the same situation of the extremists being the root cause for all these problems.

What is going on between Israel and Palestine is just another example.

Of late, we hear so many episodes of the Catholic bishops having sexually abused the minors over the years.

These are some of my reasons as to why I don't want to entertain any religion in my life anymore. I am supposed to be a Hindu by birth. In my early childhood, I too was going to the temples with my parents and relatives. My belief was that the people go to the temple to look at the idol of the deity, in this particular case, and pray to God with full attention and concentration.

But, what I witnessed in those temples made me wonder as to what is going on up there. The men and women, who were at the temple in their best possible attire, were glancing at each other exchanging smiles, instead of looking at the idol and praying. It didn't look right to me.

Besides, there were numerous occasions where I witnessed the role of the mighty MONEY and high-level contacts in the temples. If you have money or know somebody in a high level at any temple, then you don't have to wait in the long queue out in the scorching sun or pouring rain to gain entry in to the temple. You can be there inside in no time standing very close to the idol of the deity. It didn't look right to me.

So, numerous instances like these made me not blindly believe in any preaching or rituals of the religion. I truly believe in our God Almighty. As for me God is the utmost and ultimate super power that controls all the galaxies.

What does God look like? It is beyond anybody's comprehension.

Is God a he or a she or both? I have no idea.

Where is God? God is everywhere, not confined to the place of worship.

We are all God's children. This classification of whites, blacks, etc. is a man made evil set up to segregate God's children based on their skin colour. I believe that various religions were formulated primarily to induce some sort of discipline in the people's behaviour towards each other. But, here also, the men who initiated and introduced the religion wanted to convey their own vested views and beliefs as the foundation of that religion.

I may be wrong. But, I believe that the creators of the Hindu religion formulated the evil caste system that defines and describes India's rigid social system.

As per the information that I collected from one of the magazines on the Indian caste system, this system divided the society as follows:

1.   At the top are the "Brahmans," traditionally priests, who performed religious ceremonies.

2.   Then comes "Kshatriyas," traditionally warriors, who took charge of the army and government.

3.   Next comes "Vaishyas" who are traditionally farmers, craftsmen and merchants to attend to the respective responsibilities.

4.   Next comes "Shudras" who are known as the lowest recognized class working as slaves or servants. These were the poorest and the least educated of the cited four classes.

5.   Below the "Shudras" are the people who are referred to as "untouchables." These people did the work that others thought of as "unclean" like collecting garbage and waste products. I gather that these people were not allowed to live in villages but built their huts on the outskirts. If a higher caste person was touched by an untouchable or even had the shadow of one fall on him or her, that person had to go through certain ceremonies to get rid of the "pollution."

While I sincerely believe that we are all God's creation and hence his children, how can I claim myself to be a part of the religion or the system that treats one set of people as "untouchables?" According to me, it is a real disgrace. It is exactly like how some evil white men created the races to segregate certain sets of people based on their skin colour.

Mahatma Gandhi devoted almost his entire life calling on the Indians to stop this harsh treatment of "untouchables." Gandhi called these people as "Harijans" meaning "children of God." Because of his and other reformers' efforts, the 1950 Indian Constitution outlawed discrimination against these "untouchables" and provided for quota system in schools, government, and elected positions. This is similar to the "Affirmative Action" that is needed to rectify the injustice inflicted on a set of minority people. But, the customs and traditions change very slowly, especially in Indian villages. As such, a lot of "untouchables" still suffer quite a lot with this type of discrimination.

Besides, Mr. Gandhi devoted all his life for harmony between Hindus and Muslims. A right wing religious Hindu extremist, Godse, murdered Gandhi because of this.

I am proud of the fact that I was born and brought up in India where Mahatma Gandhi, the greatest leader the world has ever known, was born and brought up. **He preached, practised and proved to the world that non-violence, non-cooperation and civil disobedience would be the most powerful but peaceful weapons of mass destruction to eradicate the evil British Empire** that proclaimed, "The sun never sets in the British Empire."

I am proud of the fact that I was born and brought up in India from where quite a lot of scientists, doctors and computer specialists who contribute to the advancement of the computer technology in Silicon Valley of USA were also born and brought up. Besides, I am also proud of the fact that I was born and brought up in India that introduced, amongst other things, Yoga, Meditation and *Kama Sutra* to the world.

But, at the same time, I am really ashamed of the fact that I was born and brought up in a system that **still continues** to practise corruption, bribery, dowry, injustice to innocent people, women and "untouchables" **as an acceptable normal way of life in India**. I don't know whether this will ever change in the near future. God only knows.

I may seem, and sound like, a strange and controversial character. May be I am. But, I don't think of any harm to those who are unable to take care of themselves. So, I feel comfortable for what I am. I believe that every religion was introduced to induce and enforce some sort of discipline in a society, as conceived by the creator of that religion. As long as the followers of every religion respect and regard the belief and faith of the followers of other religions, I have no problem there. You practice what you believe in, but don't insist and impose your views and beliefs on others. They are entitled to believe and practice whatever they want to. You respect that. You live your life the way you want to and let others live their lives the way they want to. Live and let live should be the motto.

I have my own religious belief and discipline. It is basic and fundamental, straightforward and simple. It has two main guiding principles that I try to follow. **Be nice to everyone. Help whenever and wherever you can.** I expect that this is what all the religions may be preaching in principle.

I do admit the fact that I have a problem in trying to be nice to everyone, especially the extremists and the republicans. The republicans are really indifferent to the homeless, poor and innocent people who are unable to help themselves. These people are also God's children like any of us. So, they need all the help and support from us to find a decent living. This is the reason why I find it hard to be nice to the extremists and republicans.

Now let us talk about the women's role in our society. It is sad to note how selfish most men are when it comes to how their women are treated in almost every society. We men make love to our respective partners to make babies. Of course, this process is very pleasurable for both. But, from the moment the baby is conceived, who is carrying the baby, who is going through all the hardships associated with the pregnancy, who is delivering the baby, who is taking care of and bringing up the baby from day one, and who is running the household with all the cooking, cleaning, etc.? Of course, we, the men, may offer some sort of help to make things a bit easy for the women. But, still the point is, who is really and actually doing it day in and day out? Almost everywhere it is our women, not the men.

We, the men, are out at work to earn money, as we are the breadwinners for our homes. Of late, in most families, due to the soaring cost of living and the uncertain economic climate, the women are also forced to go out to work to supplement the income that men bring home on top of caring for the children and family in their daily routines. But, what do women get in return?

Of late, I heard in the news that 1/3 of the families in the USA experience spousal abuse where the women are ill treated, beaten, etc. by their male partners. How come? This is because, almost in every society the concept and tradition are, men are like the God Almighty of the household and women are there to serve them. This is nothing but male chauvinism exploiting the women in spite of every thing they do for the good of the family. Women are being referred to, in many cases, as the "weaker sex" and kept suppressed all the time. The so-called "equal respect and equal opportunity" is only on paper, not in practice mostly.

I believe, almost everywhere, the society prefers baby boy, but not baby girl. I am not all that sure as to how far this is true in the Western society. But, I know that it is definitely so in India. I have heard of cases where some illiterate women in Indian villages killing their newborn baby girls. It is sad and shocking, but it is true. Remember the dowry system in India where the bride's parents beg, borrow or steal, as they have to give dowry in some form or other to the groom's family. Why can't it be just the other way, where the groom's parents give dowry to the bride's family? No. The boys are the preferred commodities and the girls are not. Thank God, I hear that things are improving a bit on this issue mainly in cities. But, still it is in practice almost everywhere else, unfortunately.

Again, in India, the boys are not condemned that much if they mess around with different girls, because they are boys. But, if a girl does the same, that is it. The society will pounce on her, saying that she is a slut, bitch, etc. In those days, men were allowed to have more than one wife and mistresses. Can you imagine, the women having more than one husband and other lovers? My question, by quoting all these, is simply this. If a man is allowed, then why can't the same be applied to woman as well? Why this type of discrimination towards women in spite of all the sacrifices that they go through in bringing up the families?

Let me quote another recent instance on this sad state of affairs where the women are not treated fairly even by their own parents. I refer to the front-page article "Two Daughters Fight Hindu Mores for Piece Of Chutney Empire" in *The Wall Street Journal* dated February 23, 2004.

As per the report, two daughters and four sons slaved and sweated to build their father's business that was worth around $75,000,000 in 2002. Now the daughters are fighting in London Royal Court of Justice for their fair share of the business after the father's death in 1997. Their own mother contends that the shares never really belonged to the daughters in the first place since under the Hindu tradition, "the daughters of the family are never given a part of the family business." This is the argument by their own mother after she had witnessed how much her daughters contributed towards the success of the business. Can you believe it?

On a personal note, when we had our two daughters, I always wanted them to believe that "anything boys can do, girls can do better" and I am so proud they did just that. My unshakeable belief is whether it is a boy or a girl, it is our offspring, and as such each has exactly the same right and share of the property.

The "Affirmative Action" must include women also. They were also unfairly kept suppressed by men over the years for a very long time. It must stop soon for good. We see some bright and hardworking women like Oprah Winfrey, Hillary Clinton, Martha Stewart, etc. having come up in life. That is not enough. We need to see more, and accordingly we need to provide appropriate equal opportunities for them to get there. Israel, India, Indonesia, Pakistan, Sri Lanka, England, just to name a few, did have women as their Prime Ministers. What is the matter with the so-called Super Power? Don't we have competent women to become the President?

All those women who proved beyond doubt the fact that "anything boys can do, girls can do better" should be really careful and watch their backs at all times in this male dominated society. Oprah, you have two reasons to worry about, because besides the fact that you are a woman you are not white. As for Hillary, she is a democrat. God and Martha only know as to what happened regarding her conviction for lying to the investigators.

If Martha is to be sent to prison for this reason, then why don't we punish Mr. Bush, Mr. Blair and warmongering members of their administrations for their big lies to the entire world causing chaos and countless number of killings in Iraq and damage to our economy? They should be in prison for life with no parole.

Whenever anybody says anything contrary to what the right-wingers say, they brand that person immediately with contempt as the "liberal." So, not knowing the real meaning for the term "liberal," I checked in The American Heritage Dictionary the meanings for the terms "conservative" and "liberal" and this is what I found.

Conservative:
Favoring traditional views and values, tending to oppose change.

Liberal:
Not linked to or by established, traditional, orthodox, or authoritarian attitudes, views, or dogmas, free from bigotry. Favoring proposals for reform, open to

new ideas for progress, and tolerant of the ideas and behavior of others, broad minded.

Thank God, I am blessed because I am a liberal and I am proud of it. Let "the compassionate conservatives" continue to oppose changes but carry on with their traditional views and values to widely advertise and encourage "Niggers for Sale" and slavery. As for me, those people who initiated and entertained slavery are nothing but a real disgrace to the human race.

If you really believe in God, you must love and care for other human being, especially those who are unable to help themselves. Respect others like how you would like to be respected by others. Since we are all God's creation, no race or religion is superior to another race or religion. We all have different colours, features and faiths. That is all.

What needs to be done to improve the race and religious harmony? I can think of just two.

First of all, the media must stop conveying any type of message that leads to racial and religious hatred between people. For example, there should be no more screening of the programs that instigate violence and hatred towards ethnic minorities. Instead, the media should do all it can to educate the people to enhance understanding and appreciation of other races, cultures and religions. The motivation should be to improve the racial and religious harmony between all sects of people.

Another thing we can do is to encourage inter-racial and inter-religious marriages. For example, a person from one race and religious faith must be encouraged to marry a person from other race and religious faith. This will help to view the values and virtues of people without tunnel vision.

––––––––––––

Points for *Something to Think About*:

- Any discrimination based on race and religion is not only illegal, but it is immoral.

• There have been some improvements in the race relations, but still we have a long way to go in this respect.

• We are all God's children. So, we belong to just one race viz. human race.

• Initiation and introduction of races and religions were the work of a set of men with vested interests.

• In our own family, we are all different by feature and behaviour. We may not agree on everything and may argue a lot. But, we don't fight and kill each other because of this difference. We agree to disagree and learn to live together as one family. Why can't we extend this same approach beyond our family to include everyone in our community, country and other countries as well?

• We find good and bad in every race, community and country. These are not confined to any one particular race or group of people.

• Media must stop branding the blacks and Hispanics only as the suspects for any crime. Most of these thugs, including white thugs, are from the poor and broken families. The media must promote racial harmony and stop spreading hatred towards the non-whites.

• Racial hatred and discrimination are not coming just from the whites towards non-whites. Non-whites are equally to be blamed for their hatred and discrimination towards whites.

• "Let us not seek to satisfy our thirst for freedom by drinking from the cup of bitterness and hatred."

• We must do all we can to "live in a nation where they will not be judged by the colour of their skin but by the content of their character." "And if America is to be a great nation, this must come true."

• We must strive hard "to speed up that day when all of God's children, black men and white men, Jews and Gentiles, Protestants and Catholics, will be able to join hands and sing in the words of the old Negro spiritual 'Free at last! Free at last! Thank God Almighty, we are free at last.'"

• Sports arena proved to be one good area where all races share their joy and sorrow like one good family. This type of racial harmony should extend everywhere in every walk of life.

• Affirmative Action must continue in the fields of education and employment for some more time, until such time all minorities also get good education and employment opportunities.

• All the celebrities who are rich and famous, especially those from ethnic minorities, should consider setting up an establishment to provide support, guidelines and motivation to the millions of kids from under privileged families. This will help the kids to become caring future citizens instead of getting involved in violent activities.

• What really matters is how a religion is being practised, but not preached.

• Religious preachers should educate and help everyone to live harmoniously together irrespective of whatever religious faith and belief we all may have. Respect others' faith and belief like how you would like others to respect your faith and belief.

• Extremists use the religion as an excuse to get their personal and political agenda. Innocent people are being used as the pawns in their political game of chess for this purpose.

• Don't blindly believe the preaching and rituals of any religion. Use your head, common sense and reasoning.

• Every religion must give equal right and respect to all human being. Nobody is superior and nobody is inferior since we are all God's creation.

• Corruption, bribery, dowry, injustice to innocent people including women should be eradicated from every society. It is an insult and disgrace to practise any of these in a civilized society.

• The basic principles of any religion should be to be nice to everyone and to help whenever and wherever you can.

• Male chauvinism must stop. Anything boys can do, girls can do better.

• As per American Heritage Dictionary, the conservatives tend to oppose changes and favour traditional views and values.

• As per American Heritage Dictionary, the liberals are not linked to or by established, traditional, orthodox, or authoritarian attitudes, views, or dogmas, and are free from bigotry. They favour proposals for reform, open to new ideas for progress, and tolerant of the ideas and behaviour of others, and they are broad-minded.

• If you believe in God, you must love and care for other human being, especially those who are unable to help themselves.

• The media must stop conveying messages that lead to racial and religious hatred between people. Instead, it should do all it can to educate the people to enhance understanding and appreciation of other races, cultures and religions. The motivation should be to improve the racial and religious harmony between all sects of people.

• We must encourage inter racial and inter religious marriages. A person from one race and religious faith must be encouraged to marry a person from other race and religious faith. This will help to view the values and virtues of people without tunnel vision.

Working for Living

Except for the privileged few, almost all of us have to work hard for some employer or other and get paid for what we do. That is it. No more than that. You sweat day in and day out to make profit for your employer. But, you don't have any say on how the business that you are working for is run, what sort of working environment you can have, what sort of health insurance cover you can have, what sort of pension you can hope to have, etc. You just hang in there hoping and praying that you don't get laid off.

I have worked at various sites in India, England, Germany, Saudi Arabia and the USA. Almost in all the sites, the business is run to take care of the interests of the big bosses and the shareholders only. In some cases, there were some benefits given to the employees like some bonus just before Christmas. But, mostly the employees are more like slaves or robots. Just do what you are contracted to do and get paid for your work. You can't ask for anymore than that.

Please believe me, I have my utmost admirations and respect for the big bosses because of their entrepreneurial and management capabilities. They are really great, sharp, smart and shrewd in running the day-to-day activities of the business. I have my sincere and heartfelt praise for their hard work. I have no complaints on that count. My complaints and grievances are on the following grounds only towards the bosses and shareholders of the big corporations:

- They bribe and then bully the elected representatives of people's governments to take care of their special interests.
- They don't share the profit with the employees even though it is the employees who produced that profit to the employer.
- They don't include the employees in their policymaking process.
- They don't provide good working environments and conditions.
- They don't provide equal opportunities to the women in respect of the

pay and promotion.
• They exploit and exhaust all the loopholes in the laws to find ways around in respect of tax evasion.
• They have no conscience or concern for the employees' hardships while they outsource jobs and manufacturing process elsewhere. They just lay off people who worked all their lives for that business.

Let us examine each issue in detail now.

I believe, I have detailed enough information already in other chapters regarding the big businesses ruining the basic fabric of our democracy viz. *the government of the people, by the people and for the people.* The corporations control the corrupt politicians and get the laws of the land in favor of the greedy corporations. So, there is no need to dwell on this subject any further here.

The issue of not including the employees to share the profits and to participate in the policymaking process is nothing but real injustice to every working human being.

Of course, all those management personnel that contribute a lot every day towards the success of the business do deserve appropriate and reasonable proportion, **not exorbitant portion or stock options,** of the profit. They deserve it since they earned it by doing real hard and responsible work every day.

I may be wrong and ignorant in respect of the shareholders' role in the day-to-day running of the business. But, to the best of my knowledge, the shareholders don't do a damn thing for the day-to-day running of the business. They have just invested their money in the business exactly like how we invest money in savings account in banks and occasionally attend "shareholders meetings." Besides that, what is their contribution towards the day-to-day running of the company? NOTHING. As such, in my opinion, they do not deserve any big chunk of the profit while the hard working employees who sweat day in and day out do not get any share of the profit. It is true that they have invested their money. So, they are entitled to a real good return on their investment. So, as for me, they should be given a good return that is slightly higher than the best possible interest that they could hope to get elsewhere with their investment. This arrangement is nothing but fair in every sense of the word.

Then, as regards to the day to day running and policymaking process of the business, in what way the shareholders are better equipped and informed than those employees and the management personnel who work ever so hard every day for the success of the business? Only the management personnel and the employees should have any say in the policymaking process, but definitely not the shareholders.

Under the present set up and circumstances, what sort of motivation and enthusiasm can anyone expect from the employees? They just do the job like a robot, because they are getting paid for their work. Their heart and soul won't be there. Because justifiably they feel that they are not part of the success or failure of the business since they are not included in the day-to-day running and policymaking process of the business.

I gather that there are a few establishments where everyone who works for that establishment is a shareholder actively participating, through their elected representatives, to decide on the policymaking process and the day-to-day running of the business. They sincerely believe that they will sail or sink together as one team. The sense of belonging is there. As such, they put their heart and soul to make the business to succeed and make profit since they hope to share the profit. Just imagine the productivity one can hope to have when each employee puts everything he/she has towards the success of the business. Why can't every business, whether it is a small business or big corporations, be run on this share and care principles? That is what I am hoping and praying for. Is it not fair? Is it not the right way to run the business? What is preventing the employees from getting this fair deal? It is none other than the greedy, corrupt and selfish senior management and the shareholders.

As per the present set up, the senior management and the shareholders are just self-centered and greedy. They want to make more and more money using the employees' hard work, but will not give anything in return by way of bonus or profit sharing. The employees just get their basic pay. Period. This is immoral and unjust. The shareholders don't give a damn as to what happens to the welfare of the hard working employees.

As mentioned in the "Introduction" chapter, this book is all about conveying my views and thoughts on various issues. Let me make a brief mention about what I think of the stock market.

I don't know anything about the working of the stock market. All my experience has been, is that I lost quite a bit of my capital in the stock market collapse that happened in 1986. I had my savings invested through a fund manager in some managed funds. For no fault of mine, I lost considerable amount of my capital because of the collapse. What did I do wrong? Why should I lose my capital?

From what I see on the television, my impression of the stock market is that it is like a filthy fish market crowded with all types of speculators who decide on the fate of the stocks of various establishments using all types of underhand dealings and inside information. We have heard quite a number of stories on the dishonest dealings by these speculators. I don't know the basis on which these speculators mess with the values of the stocks. Irrespective of, and in spite of, all the hard work done by the employees at their work place, the stock values of their businesses are assessed and assigned by these speculators who seem to be in panic mode at all times. I always believe that good things come out of calm and clear thinking, but not out of impulsive and hasty decisions. Do it in haste and repent at leisure. I don't get it and I don't find any justice in this. What is the point in the employees working ever so hard to make profit for their business, if some outside speculators are to decide on the fortune or failure of that business? It doesn't make any sense to me.

Now, let us talk about the working environments and the conditions. In some of the sites that I worked with, I did find some real good working environments and conditions.

For example, some of these establishments had some real good fitness facilities. They had quite a number of treadmills, rowing machines, exercise bikes, flex balls, abs machines, etc. Most of the workers there did make an effective use of them before and after their working hours and also during lunch break. These facilities helped the workers to keep fit both mentally and physically. Some sites organized evening and weekend classes for Yoga, meditation and relaxation techniques, thus in turn to be more productive at work. Some sites even had a separate set of staff in the human resources department to attend to the activities of the employees' wellness club. I found that type of working environment really beneficial in the interest of everybody there. They had minimal number of time off due to minor illnesses, as the workers were both physically and mentally feeling real good. So, naturally productivity will be good too.

Some sites had a cafeteria too, where the employees can get their breakfast, lunch and even evening meals at subsidized costs. It is all to the benefit of the entire establishment.

As for the working conditions, some departments had section heads that believe in "friendly but firm" attitude in getting the things done. Every worker in those sections did their work with a happy frame of mind helping and teasing each other at all times. They enjoyed going to work, as the atmosphere was friendly.

But, at the same time, in some sites I did find some unpleasant section heads. They think that they are God Almighty and behaved like real bullies towards other workers. Their attitude had been "my way or highway." Obviously, the workers in those sections attended to the work because they have to. There was no heart or enthusiasm in his or her working routines. So, naturally productivity was just marginal.

So, in the interest of everyone especially the productivity, why can't every establishment actively consider and implement all the good things that I mentioned above and a "friendly but firm" working atmosphere?

How about the working conditions for the women?

Almost everywhere, I found that the women who did exactly the same type of work, at times with even more responsibilities, received less pay and recognition than the men who did similar jobs. The usual claim "equal opportunity employer," is nothing but just a joke and slogan in those places. I don't have to say anything more in respect of the promotional prospects for the women in most of those sites. As a result, obviously, the women were down in spirits in carrying out their duties.

Besides, we heard a lot of stories about sexual harassments in various sites, especially if the women happen to look attractive. Sometimes, the women's pay and promotional prospects depended more on how well they responded to the sexual harassments. Unfortunately, almost everywhere, it is still a male dominated working environment. Why can't people value, respect and reward a person based on what that person has between the ears, but not on what that person has between the thighs? It is male chauvinism and male domination almost everywhere. Unfortunately, still there is a long way to go even in the Western society to remedy this unpleasant atmosphere. Hope and pray that this type of injustice gets eliminated soon everywhere.

I heard about a few establishments that provided nursery facilities in the same or nearby building to young mothers who can leave their kids there with a happy frame of mind. It is an excellent idea. Why can't all the employers look into this aspect and implement the same effectively?

Now let us consider the cases where the corrupt corporations exploit all the loopholes to avoid paying the taxes that are due to the government. I would request the readers to checkout the website cited herein for a detailed staggering report on this subject.

I copy below just a few sections of the report for ready reference.

As per, *http://www.commondreams.org/views03/0228-10.htm,*

"As readers might imagine, this double accounting is not available to working Americans. But it is available to corporations, who use this double accounting to avoid paying the taxes they legitimately owe the government. The Joint Committee on Taxation of the U.S. Congress has concluded that corporations use differences between tax rules and accounting rules to avoid paying taxes on their profits. Take Enron, for example. Enron reported to its shareholders that it earned $3.625 billion in profit between 1996 and 2000. It then turned around and reported to the IRS that it had only earned $76 millions in profit during those years. This double accounting defrauded tens of thousands of shareholders and pensioners out of billions of dollars, for the cooked books were discovered to have masked questionable investment procedures.

What is not widely known, however, is that Enron's reported profits should have generated $1.142 billion in taxes – yet the corporation paid only $63million in those years.

This is a scandal that is in no way limited to Enron alone, or to a handful of rogue companies who keep double books and in the process defraud the government of money owed for taxes.

In a remarkable study, Harvard University economist Mihir A. Desai has calculated the difference between the profits that corporations reported to the Internal Revenue Service in 1998, and the profits that accountants certified in the annual reports the companies issued to their stockholders. The difference between them is staggering: $154 billion in 1998. The result of almost one-sixth of a trillion dollars hidden by accountants' sleight-of-hand from the IRS? The federal government did not collect $54 billion that should have been paid in taxes.

How do these corporations get away with two sets of books? How can they tell their stockholders they are raking in profits, and then turn around and tell the IRS that they had such a bad year that they will pay little or nothing in taxes?

According to the New York Times, the IRS has recently reported that while small corporations bear their fair share of taxes, large corporations don't. Though the corporate tax rate is 35 percent, the IRS found that the 10,000 largest corporations paid only 20.3 percent of their 1999 profits in federal income taxes. The second tier of companies, good sized but not large, paid taxes at a rate almost 50 percent greater, 30.9 percent. And here's the kicker: the 10,000 largest corporations had over 25 times the total profits that the second tier generated – and got away with paying at a lesser rate even though they earned a lot more. That is not progressive taxation – it is regressive taxation.

By what means do corporations evade paying taxes on their profits? Tax shelters allow fake losses (think of all Enron's "deals"), deductions are double accounted, and cash is transferred internally. Corporations claim excess depreciation or reinvest earnings abroad to shield them from domestic taxation.

All those stock options we have been reading about? They not only weaken corporations and bilk stockholders, it turns out they divert a huge amount of tax revenue away from the IRS and into the pockets of wealthy corporate executives. CEOs get rich not only at the expense of stockholders, but at the expense of taxpayers: when corporations do not pay what they owe, the bill comes due to the rest of us, either in higher taxes or in a mounting national debt that our children will have to repay.

The problem is getting worse. Professor Desai found that in those same years, 1996 through 2000, the value of stock options awarded more than sextupled, from $32 billion to more than $199 billion. The value of stock options that were exercised – actually used – more than tripled, to $106 billion. $78 billion in options were exercised in the nation's 150 largest firms alone, with a resulting ratio of options exercised to operating cash flow of over 29 percent. Corporate profits, and the taxes that should be paid on those profits, are flooding into the investment portfolios and bank accounts of corporate executives."

Please checkout *http://www.corpwatch.org/news/PND.jsp?articleid=5539* for a report on "Congressional Panel Finds Outrageous Enron Pay Deals, Tax Evasion"

"Enron's failure destroyed the retirement savings of thousands of employees and hurt individual investors and pension funds nationwide. It was the first in a series of big company scandals that shook public confidence in the stock market and the integrity of corporate America."

Please don't forget the link that had been there for a long time between the Bush family and the big bosses at Enron.

Also, please checkout *http://www.wsws.org/articles/2003/aug2003/preo-a19_prn.shtml* for a report on "Bush grants permanent legal immunity to US corporations looting Iraqi oil." As per this site,

"An extraordinary Presidential Executive Order, signed into law by President Bush on May 22 but kept out of the pages of the US media, further underscores the real motivations behind the illegal US-led invasion and occupation of Iraq.

Ostensibly drawn up in order to protect Iraq's oil wealth, Executive Order (EO) 13303, "Protecting the Development Fund for Iraq and Certain Other Property in Which Iraq Has an Interest," provides unlimited authority for US corporations to loot Iraqi oil and grants them permanent immunity from any legal actions over the consequences."

"In terms of legal liability," Divine's report began, "the Executive Order cancels the concept of corporate accountability and abandons the rule of law."

"The EO means that American oil companies operating in Iraq are now completely immune from legal accountability. If they carry out environmental destruction, oil spills or labor rights violations, no one affected will have any legal recourse. In addition, the EO eliminates the potential for any future Iraqi government to sue US oil companies for compensation and damages. The GAP report describes it as "a licence for corporations to loot Iraq and its citizens."

The EO exempts US oil companies operating in Iraq not only from international law, but from American civil and criminal liability as well. It renders any commercial activity within the US involving Iraqi oil exempt from judicial accountability. Devine notes that this legal exemption covers everything from laws concerning workplace safety, minimum wage requirements, environmental protection and consumer fraud.
Also overridden are the normal accountability requirements relating to US corporations in receipt of government contracts. US administrative law enforces a raft of conditions for the awarding and administration of US government contracts in areas such as competitive bidding, labour conditions, and open accounting standards. None of these will now be enforceable for contracts involving Iraqi oil, giving the Bush administration a free hand in its relations with companies such as Halliburton and Bechtel. As Devine noted, "the EO is a blank check for pork barrel spending."

For a report on "George W. Bush on Corporations," please checkout, *http://www.issues2000.org/Celeb/George_W_Bush_Corporations.html*,

"Ken Lay and Enron were Bush's leading supporters, contributing $113,800 directly to his campaign and another $888,265 to the Republican

National Committee, an arm of the campaign, according to the Center for Responsive Politics. Bush repaid Lay and other "Pioneers"--those who raised $100,000 or more for his campaign--with his shameful tax plan. He continues to push for a stimulus plan that benefits corporations over workers. He is pressing Congress to pass the Enron energy plan, which features massive subsidies to energy companies and further deregulation."

Sorry, I don't want to go any further on the tax evasions by corporations and the collaborations between the corporations and the Bush Administration. It makes me sick. These topics are the subject matters by themselves for some separate books by the experts in these fields.

Now, let us talk about the corporations "offshore tax evasion" process and outsourcing of jobs overseas.

As per, http://www.uaw.org/solidarity/rnews/03/q1/r3/r3q1_2.html,

"With the White House and both houses of Congress now controlled by people who, for the most part, push the corporate agenda with free trade agreements and more government supports for private companies and fewer supports for people, what happens now?

The president and Congress are going to be even more anti-worker and anti-labor than they have been for the past two years. The team act, comp time, national right to work, paycheck deception and bonus bill might all resurface."

As per, http://lists.iww.org/pipermail/alerts/2003-October/000450.html,

"Some corporate leaders are trying every trick to reduce paying their fair share of taxes in an effort to boost their profits. Last December, Congress' Joint Committee on Taxation reported that corporate tax loopholes and tax breaks for this year will total $843 billion! (In 1965, the percentage of taxes corporations paid for U.S. federal, state, and local taxes amounted to 4.1% of U.S. Gross Domestic Product (GDP), and today it has fallen to only 1.2 percent of GDP.)

This particular tax loophole allows corporations to stage sham transactions and fake corporate relocation to establish a "paper" office—for tax purposes only—in offshore tax and regulatory havens.

Given America's current record-high budget deficits, the $4 billion lost to this loophole translates into fewer children in Head Start, fewer school teachers and higher taxes for working Americans."

The North American Alliance for Fair Employment (NAFFE) is a network of organizations concerned about the growth of contingent work.

Its background briefing paper, "Workers and Politicians Must Challenge Corporations' Global Hiring Strategy" argues for a global strategy to counter outsourcing and offshoring strategy that pits workers against each other. It identifies seven components of such a strategy, including the global promotion of labor rights, and the creation of an effective social safety net.

I request the readers to checkout this important report that is given in PDF format. This report is about corporations moving tens of thousands of white collar and service jobs to low-wage countries. It can be checked out and printed from the site, *http://www.fairjobs.org/docs/jobflight.pdf. Also, please checkout http://www.ips-dc.org/reports/top200text.htm* for a report on "Top 200: The Rise of Corporate Global Power."

KEY FINDINGS

1. Of the 100 largest economies in the world, 51 are corporations; only 49 are countries (based on a comparison of corporate sales and country GDPs).
2. The Top 200 corporations' sales are growing at a faster rate than overall global economic activity. Between 1983 and 1999, their combined sales grew from the equivalent of 25.0 percent to 27.5 percent of World GDP.
3. The Top 200 corporations' combined sales are bigger than the combined economies of all countries minus the biggest 10.
4. The Top 200s' combined sales are 18 times the size of the combined annual income of the 1.2 billion people (24 percent of the total world population) living in "severe" poverty.
5. While the sales of the Top 200 are the equivalent of 27.5 percent of world economic activity, they employ only 0.78 percent of the world's workforce.

6. Between 1983 and 1999, the profits of the Top 200 firms grew 362.4 percent, while the number of people they employ grew by only 14.4 percent.
7. A full 5 percent of the Top 200s' combined workforce is employed by Wal-Mart, a company notorious for union-busting and widespread use of part-time workers to avoid paying benefits. The discount retail giant is the top private employer in the world, with 1,140,000 workers, more than twice as many as No. 2, DaimlerChrysler, which employs 466,938.
8. U.S. corporations dominate the Top 200, with 82 slots (41 percent of the total). Japanese firms are second, with only 41 slots.
9. Of the U.S. corporations on the list, 44 did not pay the full standard 35 percent federal corporate tax rate during the period 1996-1998. Seven of the firms actually paid less than zero in federal income taxes in 1998 (because of rebates). These include: Texaco, Chevron, PepsiCo, Enron, Worldcom, McKesson and the world's biggest corporation—General Motors.
10. Between 1983 and 1999, the share of total sales of the Top 200 made up by service sector corporations increased from 33.8 percent to 46.7 percent. Gains were particularly evident in financial services and telecommunications sectors, in which most countries have pursued deregulation.

The site *http://www.globalissues.org/TradeRelated/Corporations/Evasion.asp* has quite a lot of information that I want the readers to read and hence I copied the text version of it ("Evasion of Responsibilities and Dues") at the end of this chapter. I very much request the readers to check it out to realize the impact of this evil empire on each and every one of us.

The site, http://news.com.com/2100-1001-976828.html gives an excellent report on 'U.S. firms move IT overseas'. It is another eye opener.

The site, http://www.commondreams.org/cgibin/print.cgi?file=/headlines03/0527-08.htm gives a good report on "Offshore Companies Do $1 Billion in Business with US Government"

Okay, we browsed through quite a bit of information on what the big corporations are up to and its impact on every one of us including our future generations because of the ever-increasing national debt.

But, now the question is, what do you want to do about it?

First of all, do you want to do something positive about improving your working conditions, pay, participation in profit sharing and policy making in respect of how your business is run, etc.?

If the answer is "NO," then just go back to your armchair, turn on and watch your favorite television program. Be indifferent to your present and future living conditions and the future of your future generations.

But, if the answer is "YES," then first of all check your employment contract to find out whether there is any clause that will fire you if you try to follow any peaceful remedial course of action to uplift your working conditions. I am positive you should be able to take positive action to fight for your rights peacefully. NO VIOLENCE at any cost and at any time.

Discreetly find out how many of other co-workers feel the way you feel and want to do something about it.

If need be, persuade others to embark on taking remedial measures. Having done that, if you have quite a number of people with similar passion and perseverance to take action **peacefully**, consult with each other and arrive at appropriate peaceful measures such as work-to-rule, peaceful protest sit-ins, march, etc. Only you know the details of what you can and you can't do in this regard. Persevere in your efforts. Please remember, **NO VIOLENCE of any sort**. If you have determination, devotion and dedication in this context, you will succeed. Don't forget what Gandhi did in India. If he was able to get rid of the evil British Empire from India using peaceful approach only, then you guys should be able to persuade your employer to give you what you are entitled to. Good Luck. That is all I can say regarding your personal employment and working conditions.

But, there is another simple and straightforward means to get justice to everyone. All this needs is to eradicate the bricks and bones of the big corporations' evil empire. Who are these bricks and bones? It is none other than each and every elected republican from top to bottom in local, state and federal levels.

Let me convey my reasons as to why every poor, low and middle-income group hard working citizens should eradicate these republicans for good.

The big corporations and the special interest groups control the local, state and federal governments. The root cause for this serious problem is the campaign contributions and the bullying by the lobbyists. Nobody can deny this.

Who is opposing to introduce the laws that will eradicate this menace for good? Republicans.

Who keeps close ties with and receives more money from the big corporations? Republicans.

Who enacted the laws to give massive tax cut to the wealthiest people of America? Republicans.

Who is providing more government supports to private companies, but little or no support to ordinary hard working taxpayers of America? Republicans.

The republicans control all the three branches of the federal government.

Who is doing NOTHING to prevent the big corporations from moving tens of thousands of jobs and services to overseas? Republicans.

Who is refusing to enact laws that will prohibit the federal government contracts to the corporations that relocate to overseas just to avoid due share of the tax? Republicans.

Who enacted the Executive Order 13303 granting legal immunity to US Corporations looting Iraqi oil? Republicans.

Who created and nurtured the monster Saddam in the 1980s? Republicans.

Who lied to the entire world claiming immediate and imminent threat from Saddam and invaded Iraq for oil and global domination? Republicans.

Who is the reason for the ever-increasing national debt because of the Iraq war, massive tax cut to the rich and the recent Medicare prescription bill? Republicans.

Who was hiding the real cost estimate of the Medicare prescription bill to the Congress and the public? Who threatened Rick Foster, in this respect, not to tell Congress the fact that the price tag would be well above the White House's stated 400 billion along with the severe warning "the consequences for insubordination are extremely severe?" Republicans.

Who is responsible for giving uncontested rebuilding contracts at the taxpayers' expense to the big corporations who were generous with their campaign contributions to the republicans? Republicans.

Who is responsible for the ever-increasing number of deaths and serious injuries to our soldiers and the innocent Iraqi civilians? Republicans.

Who is responsible for the ever-increasing national debt that needs to be paid by the present taxpayers and our future generations? Republicans.

Who is likely to follow Greenspan's recommendations to cut the social security benefits to the retirees? Republicans.

Who is opposing to enact laws to raise the basic minimum wage to the poor? Republicans.

Who did all the electoral fraud in Florida Election in 2000? Republicans.

Who managed to stop the recounting of the disputed votes in Florida? Republicans.

Who wasted enormous sum of taxpayers' money and valuable legislative time with a view to derail Clintons? Republicans.

The Senate did not approve all the Bush's judicial nominees. What did the republicans do?

They wasted quite a lot of legislative time by way of protest and then subsequently through the executive order appointed those judicial candidates.

I can go on and on to justify why the republicans should be eradicated from the people's government everywhere in local, state, and federal levels. We hear so much about the effort to get rid of Mr. Bush from the White House. It is true that this selected, but not elected, President should be removed. No doubt about it. It is a must. If you are not convinced yet in this respect, please see the award winning film documentary "Fahrenheit 9/11" that provides all the factual account justifying this necessary course of action. But, it is not enough just to stop there. It is equally important to eradicate every republican from the government since the republicans are the pillars of the big corporations. It is exactly like the scenario of Saddam and his Ba'ath Party. Both should go at the same time.

So, this option is pretty simple and easy to execute. In this case, this is what we must remember to do.

- Come what may, every eligible voter MUST carefully consider his/her choice of candidates and vote.
- Educate everyone, you know of, the importance of voting for the right candidates.
- Do all you can to persuade every eligible voter in your community to vote without failure.
- Help in anyway you can to ensure 100% voter turnout from your neighborhood.

I gave enough justifications above as regards to whom NOT to vote. Okay, whom to vote, then?

The British people have a third party, Liberal Democrats, and it has no extreme views on either side of the political spectrum. But, unfortunately, we don't have a third party like that in the USA. The ensuing election is expected to be a real close call in every aspect. As such, no real and useful purpose will be served if you waste your valuable vote on any independent candidate since it won't help to get rid of the problems that are purely due to the republicans.

So, the reality now is, we have to choose between the two evils. **The only**

option we are left with is to vote for the democrats who are lesser of the two evils. **IF** and when it happens, I am confident that the country won't be in such a big mess like how it is now. It will bring back some sort of hope for better living conditions for the poor, low and middle-income group of people. Most of us are in this group. So, we can hope to have a better future with the democrats than with the republicans in power.

But, whatever you may do, in the interest of all the hard working citizens and our future generations, ___DO NOT VOTE FOR ANY REPUBLICAN,___ **top to bottom anywhere in any local or state or federal level governments.**

Please use your head and common sense. This will be a very crucial election to decide our fate and future. Don't screw it up again and regret it later like how you did last time. Learn from the past mistakes and get it right this time.

Please do like what the British people did in the previous two elections. They eradicated the right wing extremists. But, this time they should teach a lesson to Mr. Blair as well for what he did against the wishes of the majority of the people. So, I sincerely hope and pray that they will bring the third party to power this time teaching a lesson to the other two parties.

The British public are pretty good and balanced in this respect. In Britain, the politicians can fool some people all the time, all the people sometime, but definitely not all the people all the time. British people won't have it. They are too smart for that. I wish I could say the same about us, here in the USA. I am sorry. I don't see any sign of it, because we don't seem to think through the repercussions of letting the power rest in the hands of the republicans.

Points for _Something To Think About_:

- Most of us sweat day in and day out to make profit for our employer. But, we can't share the profit that we produce and have no say on how our business is run, the type of working environment we have, type of health insurance cover we can have, type of pension we can hope to have, etc.

• Almost everywhere the business is run to take care of the interests of the big bosses and the shareholders only, but not the hard working employees.

• The big corporations bribe and bully the elected representatives of the people's governments to take care of the interests of the corporations, but not the people.

• No equal opportunities to the women with respect to pay and promotion.

• The big corporations exploit and exhaust all the loopholes in the laws to find ways around towards tax evasion.

• The big corporations have no conscience or concern towards the employees' hardships while they outsource jobs and services elsewhere and lay off the workers who worked there all their lives.

• The shareholders take a big chunk of the profit and participate in the policy making process in spite of the fact that they don't really contribute anything towards the day-to-day running of the business.

 • Almost everywhere, it is still a male dominated work environment. Sometimes, the women's pay and promotional prospects depend on how well they respond to the sexual harassments by their bosses.

• Many corporations use the differences between tax rules and the accounting rules to avoid paying taxes on their profits.

• The stock options not only weaken the corporations and bilk the stockholders, but also divert a huge amount of tax revenue away from the IRS and into the pockets of wealthy corporate executives. The CEOs get rich not only at the expense of the stockholders, but at the expense of the taxpayers. When corporations don't pay what they owe, the bill comes due to the rest of us, either in higher taxes or in a mounting national debt that our children will have to repay.

• Mr. Bush's Executive Order (EO) 13303 provides an unlimited authority for the US corporations to loot Iraqi oil and grants them permanent immunity from any legal actions over the consequences. This EO means that the American oil companies operating in Iraq are now completely immune from any legal accountability. If they carry out environmental destruction, oil spills or labour rights violations, no one affected will have any legal recourse. In addition, the EO eliminates the potential for any future Iraqi government to sue US oil companies for compensation and damages. Who are these big corporations? None other than those who got uncontested contracts in return for the big campaign contributions they made to the republicans.

• This tax loophole allows corporations to stage sham transactions and fake corporate relocation to establish a "paper" office--for tax purposes only--in offshore tax and regulatory havens.

• Of the U.S. corporations on the list of Top 200 Corporation, 44 did not pay the full standard 35 percent federal corporate tax rate during the period 1996-1998. Seven of the firms actually paid less than zero in federal income taxes in 1998 (because of rebates). These include: Texaco, Chevron, PepsiCo, Enron, WorldCom, McKesson and the world's biggest corporation—General Motors.

• For all the reasons cited above in this chapter and in the interest of all the hard working citizens and our future generations, please do not consider voting for any republican, top to bottom anywhere in any local or state or federal level governments.

Evasion of Responsibilities and Dues
by Anup Shah
This Page Last Updated Monday, August 19, 2002
The URL of this page is: *http://www.globalissues.org/TradeRelated/ Corporations/Evasion.asp*.

As various corporations improve their profits and become increasingly wealthy and powerful, the owners and leaders naturally wish to ensure ways to protect and continue the systems that have given them these possibilities. Throughout history, power play and politics has resulted in the elite of the time to institute policies that will allow them to benefit. Often, it won't benefit the majority and if it does, it is only because it doesn't impact the elite negatively. Trade wars, cold wars and hot wars have resulted over acquisition of wealth and resources and the maintenance of the hegemonic structures. The Cold War, for example, was partly about maintaining old centers of capital against other rising centers. World War I and II were also wars between imperial powers over wealth and resources.

Today, some multinational corporations wield considerable wealth, power and influence. Indeed, some of the larger corporations have more power and influence than many nations[1].

This web page has the following sub-sections:

Corporate Welfare

Corporations and corporate-funded think tanks, media and other institutions are often the ones that loudly cry at the shame of welfare and the sin of living off the government and how various social programs should be but back due to their costs. (Usually the poorest of the poor are recipients of some sort of government assistance, if it exists at all. It is usually not enough for most people. In developing countries, for example, harsh IMF, World Bank-imposed structural adjustment policies[2] mean even more cut backs on public expenditure, where the poor get his the hardest.) What is less known though is the amount of welfare that corporations receive; it is more than what citizens receive.

Corporate welfare is the break that corporations get both legally and illegally through things like subsidies, government (i.e. public) bailouts, tax incentives and so on. Corporations can influence various governments to foster a more favorable environment for them to invest in. Often, under the threat of moving elsewhere, poorer countries are forced to lower or even nearly eliminate certain corporate taxes to these large foreign investors. (This does not help lead to the level playing field that pro corporate-globalization advocates claim.)

Corporate Crime

When we talk about crime, we think of the violations of law caused by individuals, some of which are horrendous. However, almost rarely talked about (especially in corporate-owned media) is the level of crime caused by corporations. Such crime includes evasion of taxes, fraud, ignoring environmental regulations, violating labor rights, supporting military and other oppressive regimes to prevent dissent from workers, including violent crime against workers, and so on.

In the US, for example, one professor estimates that corporate crime costs the country about $200 billion a year[3].

Side Note:

Since writing the above two paragraphs originally when this page was created, the issue of corporate crime, in the U.S. particularly has taken on a whole new dimension. Events after September 11, 2001, have highlighted massive corporate failures and controversies all the way up to the President. While for now it is beyond the scope of this page to discuss all those issues (though some points are made below, as well as additional links), Benjamin Barber, professor of Political Philosophy is worth quoting, as he highlights as important issues:

"But business malfeasance ... arises from a failure of the instruments of democracy, which have been weakened by three decades of market fundamentalism, privatization ideology and resentment of government.... The truth is that runaway capitalists, environmental know-nothings, irresponsible accountants, amoral drug runners and antimodern terrorists all flourish because we have diminished the power of the public sphere. By privatizing government functions and refusing to help create democratic institutions of global governance, America has relinquished its authority to control these forces."
—Benjamin R. Barber, A Failure of Democracy, Not Capitalism[4], New York Times, July 29, 2002

Barber is highlighting that even in the most freest of societies, the United States, corporate influences have been so strong as to undermine fundamental democratic principles.

Before and since September 11, various companies and ordinary employees, shareholders and others have suffered because of accounting irregularities being highlighted, that showed that inflated stocks and other estimates of the company's status were seriously wrong. More than just a few "rotten apples" that various economists and business elite tried to describe as the cause, is the system itself[5]. As the previous link also points out, the systemic problems had long contributed to inequality and other problems, but now that even other aspects are being affected, it is now highlighting the deeper problems even more:

"The crisis is not the result of a few bad apples. The entire barrel is rotten. In this case, the barrel is the framework of rules and regulations for business. Not every executive is a fraud or cheat, but if the system permits cooking the books, defrauding investors, overcompensating executives, rigging prices, polluting the environment, breaking unions and abusing workers, then it puts pressure on every business to move in those directions. The failures of the much-vaunted U.S. model of deregulated cowboy capitalism were already evident in growing inequality and insecurity and a declining quality of life. Now even much of the positive side - growth, profits, new businesses, productivity, soaring stock markets - has been called into question as an accounting chimera. It's time to question the whole model - lock, stock and barrel."
— David Moberg, 10 Lessons from the Corporate Collapse[6], In These Times, August 16, 2002

Tax Avoidance

Through offshore tax havens and fraud, and through transfer pricing, billions of dollars go untaxed. Estimates range from $50 billion to $200 billion of revenue losses. Oxfam for example, in a report on tax havens[7], makes a "conservative estimate, [that] tax havens have contributed to revenue losses for developing countries of at least US$50 billion a year. To put this figure in context, it is roughly equivalent to annual aid flows to developing countries." And they stress that this is a conservative estimate, as it "does not take into account outright tax evasion, corporate practices such as transfer pricing, or the use of havens to under-report profit."

Individuals too have been involved in huge amounts of capital diversions. For example, former dictator of Nigeria, Sani Abacha, and his associates are said to have diverted over $55 billion to private accounts in foreign banks -- Nigeria currently suffers a $31 billion external debt burden.

Transfer Pricing -- Intercepting Wealth

Transfer pricing provides a multinational corporations' tax-avoiding dream. It allows the ability to set up offshore accounts and paper companies through which most transactions occur, without having to pay as much taxes.

Internal accounting and costing is therefore adjusted to minimize the costs and maximize the profits.

Much needed revenue for social needs in a country is therefore lost this way.

The following quotes summarize this quite well:

"The post-Second World War period witnessed not merely a rise in TNCs' control of world trade, but also growth of trade within related enterprises of a given corporation, or "intra-company" trade. While intra-company trade in natural resource products has been a feature of TNCs since before 1914, such trade in intermediate products and services is mainly a phenomenon of recent decades. By the 1960s, an estimated one-third of world trade was intra-company in nature, a proportion which has remained steady to the present day. The absolute level and value of intra-company trade has increased considerably since that time, however. Moreover, 80 per cent of international payments for technology royalties and fees are made on an intra-company basis."

—A Brief History of TNC's[8], CorpWatch.org

(Note in the above quote at the sheer amount of intra-company trade as a percentage of world trade. Bear this in mind the next time corporate-media talk about the growing trade and prosperity for all.)

"In this continuing battle over the world's wealth, "transfer pricing" becomes a crucial aspect in the interception of the wealth of both Third World and First World countries. The multinationals either manufacture in a low-wage country or purchase cheaply from a local producer. The product, is then, theoretically, routed to an offshore corporation and invoiced (billed) at that low price. There the export invoice is increased to just under the selling price of local producers. However, the offshore company is nothing more than a mailing address and a plaque on the door. No products touch that offshore entity; even the paperwork is done in corporate home offices.

"In 1980, there were eleven thousand such corporations registered in the Cayman Islands alone, which has a population of only ten thousand. [Many of these funnel a lot of money out of Central and South America] ... These corporations are doubly insulated from accountability. ...

"These secret maneuvers of multinationals, and the huge blocks of uncontrolled international finance capital, make many of the statistics on world trade questionable. **If the sales of offshore American production facilities had been treated as exports, the 1986 American trade deficit of $144 billion would have become a trade surplus of $57 billion.** (Emphasis Added)"

—J.W. Smith, The World's Wasted Wealth 2, (Institute for Economic Democracy, 1994), p. 138.

As an example of this, the following is about Rupert Murdoch's News Corporation:

"In March 1999, the Economist reported that in the four years to 30 June of the previous year, News Corporation and its subsidiaries paid an effective tax rate of only around 6 per cent. This compared with 31 per cent paid by Disney. The Economist notes that "basic corporate-tax rates in Australia, America and Britain, the three main countries in which News Corporation operates, are 36%, 35% and 30% respectively.""

"The article points to the difficulties of finding out about the specifics of News Corporations' tax affairs because of the company's complex corporate structure. "In its latest accounts, the group lists roughly 800 subsidiaries, including some 60 incorporated in such tax havens as the Cayman Islands, Bermuda, the Netherlands Antilles and the British Virgin Islands, where the secrecy laws are as attractive as the climate.""

The article continues, "This structure, dictated by Mr. Murdoch's elaborate tax planning has some bizarre consequences. The most profitable of News Corporation's British operations in the 1990s was not the Sunday Times, or its successful satellite television business, BSkyB. It was News Publishers, a company incorporated in Bermuda. News Publishers has, in the seven years to June 30th 1996, made around 1.6 billion in net profit. This is a remarkable feat for a company that seems not to have employees, nor any obvious source of income from outside Mr. Murdoch's companies."

—Tax Havens; Releasing the hidden billions for poverty eradication[2], Oxfam, June 2000

Effects of Corporate Evasion of Responsibilities
One of the quotes above, is from J.W. Smith. Wherein he describes the cost of transfer-pricing. He goes on to explain quite well the effects and points out that both high-wage and low-wage countries lose out as the wealth is siphoned to offshore accounts to avoid taxes. This is "historical mercantilism to perfection" by intercepting both the foreign country's wealth and one's own.

However, as he goes on to point out, there is a difference in that today's corporations don't have any loyalty to any nation, due to greed.

The last 20 years has seen the wealth of the United States reduced as corporations seek out[10] cheaper and cheaper places where wages are cheaper and environmental, safety and other regulatory measures are less or non-existent. (This has the effect of depressing wages and labor rights in industrialized as well as developing countries and therefore affects the wealth of those countries.)

Disparities between the wealthy and poor continue to rise, in the most powerful nation as well as all other countries. As Smith continues to point out, "Looking only at their bottom line, and listening to their own rhetoric, the managers of capital are unaware they are moving society back towards the wealth discrepancies of the early Industrial Revolution; this return to quasi-aristocratic privileges is a recipe for eventual contraction of commerce and destruction of their own wealth along with that of labor."

—J.W. Smith, The World's Wasted Wealth 2, (Institute for Economic Democracy, 1994), pp. 164-165.

While Smith wrote the above in 1994, it is applicable today as well, with the recent wave of news about "corporate crime" and fascination of some CEOs and other executives as some major American companies have faced bankruptcy or have collapsed. Yet, the media, while offering an outpouring of news and analysis have by and large concentrated on individual characters and looked for scapegoats (CEOs being the current flavor!). The impacts of the underlying system itself has been less discussed and when it has, often been described as basically ok, but just affected by a few "bad apples." As media critic Norman Solomon describes,

On the surface, media outlets are filled with condemnations of avarice. The July 15 edition of *Newsweek* features a story headlined "Going After Greed," complete with a full-page picture of George W. Bush's anguished face. But after multibillion-dollar debacles from Enron to WorldCom, the usual media messages are actually quite equivocal -- wailing about greedy CEOs while piping in a kind of hallelujah chorus to affirm the sanctity of the economic system that empowered them.

...Corporate theology about "the free enterprise system" readily acknowledges bad apples while steadfastly denying that the barrels are rotten. ... ("Let's hold people responsible -- not institutions," a recent Wall Street Journal column urged.)

...Basic questions about wealth and poverty -- about economic relations that are glorious for a few, adequate for some and injurious for countless others -- remain outside the professional focus of American journalism. In our society, prevalent inequities are largely the results of corporate function, not corporate dysfunction. But we're encouraged to believe that faith in the current system of corporate capitalism will be redemptive.

—Norman Solomon, Renouncing Sins Against the Corporate Faith[11], Media Beat, Fairness and Accuracy In Reporting, July 11, 2002

Government Interference or Assistance?

In some countries, the business community shouts a lot about government interference (in their profits) and recommends that the government be reduced in bureaucracy. While many governments are plagued with inefficiency, some is due to the powerplay of groups including various industries.

However, without the various governments, entire industries and market economies wouldn't have got started in the first place. In the US, for example:

• The pharmaceutical industry received research and development funds from the US government.
• The Internet was created with public funds, but is now handed to corporations to profit from.
• Most major industries receive some support or bailout, including:
  o Energy industries
  o Agriculture
  o Biotechnology
  o Information Technology
  o Telecommunications
  o Weapons/arms/military industrial complex
  o and so on.

While the private companies profit, any costs, such as social problems resulting from environmental degradation, resulting social degradation and so on, are all socialized. "Privatizing profits, socializing costs" is a common phrase heard in critical circles.

And politics has gotten even murkier since the aftermath of the September 11, 2001 terrorist attacks on the U.S. Some industries have used the September 11th incident to say that has led to loss of business and to try and ask for government assistance as a result. While it has surely had an effect, for example, in the airline industry, as the UK's BBC 24 news program on September 27, 2001 at about 8:30pm in an interview, said that before the tragic terrorist attacks some of the airline companies such as British Airways were already suffering quite badly, and this tragedy provided an excuse to get out of it. Of course, this doesn't mean all companies were using the excuse, but it does highlight the difficulty of addressing these issues during highly emotional times. Companies are understandably going to try and use this to their advantage if possible, to a limit.

Economist and professor at M.I.T., Paul Krugman highlights this with the case of the highly publicized Enron collapse, in a piece that appeared in the *New York Times*, quoting here at length:

Enron's illusion of profitability rested largely on "mark to market" accounting. The company entered into contracts that would yield profits, if at all, only over a number of years. But Enron jumped the gun: it treated the capitalized value of those hypothetical future gains as a current profit, which could then be used to justify high stock prices, big bonuses for executives, and so on.

...the Bush administration has turned to the political equivalent of another increasingly common accounting trick: the "one-time charge."

According to Investopedia.com, one-time charges are "used to bury unfavorable expenses or investments that went wrong." That is, instead of admitting that it has been doing a bad job, management claims that bad results are caused by extraordinary, unpredictable events: "We're making lots of money, but we had $1 billion in special expenses associated with our takeover of XYZ Corporation." And of course extraordinary events do happen; the trick is to make the most of them, as a way of evading responsibility. (Some companies, such as Cisco, have a habit of incurring "one-time charges" over and over again.)

The events of Sept. 11 shocked and horrified the nation; they also presented the Bush administration with a golden opportunity to bury its previous misdeeds. Has more than $4 trillion of projected surplus suddenly evaporated into thin air? Pay no attention to the tax cut: it's all because of the war on terrorism.

—Paul Krugman, Bush's Aggressive Accounting[12], New York Times, February 5, 2002

More Information
I have not even scratched the surface of this issue here, as it is large and complex. Since the September 11 tragedy, this issue has ballooned incredibly and I have hardly discussed any of the issues arising since then. However, there are a number of organizations doing more research on this, and critics have pointed out these issues for a long time. You could start off at the following links to learn more:
- "Tax Havens; Releasing the hidden billions for poverty eradication[13]" from Oxfam.
- "Rollback[14]" by Noam Chomsky.

- "Global Shell Games; How the corporations operate tax free[15]" by U.S. Senator Byron Dorgan.
- Corporate Welfare Information Center[16] provides a lot of links to other sources and articles.
- Corporate Welfare[17] from the Banneker Center.
- Stop Corporate Welfare![18] by Ralph Nader, Fall 1996.
- "Corporate Welfare and Foreign Policy[19]" from Foreign Policy in Focus looks at the US roles in corporate welfare, providing statistics and a collection of articles.
- Essential Information[20] has a lot of information on all sort of issues relating to corporate accountability.
- EnronGate[21] from Alternet.org news web site is an example of many sites providing articles on Enron-related issues
- Explosive Revalation$[22], from In These Times magazine, provides a look at a banking system that secretly moves trillions of dollars around the world.
- ZNet Econ Watch[23] provides analysis, news and information with a primary focus on the US Economy.

Online Sources:

(Note that listed here are only those hyperlinks to other articles from other web sites or elsewhere on this web site. Other sources such as journal, books and magazines, are mentioned above in the original text. Please also note that links to external sites are beyond my control. They might become unavailable temporarily or permanently since you read this, depending on the policies of those sites, which I cannot unfortunately do anything about.)

1. Facts.asp

2. Structural Adjustment -- A Major Cause of Poverty, http://www.globalissues.org/TradeRelated/SAP.asp
3. Ralph Nader, "It's Time to End Corporate Welfare As We Know It," Earth Island Journal, Vol. 11, No. 4, Fall 1996, http://www.earthisland.org/eijournal/new_articles.cfm?articleID=341&journalID=57
4. http://www.nytimes.com/2002/07/29/opinion/29BARB.html?todaysheadlines=&pagewanted=print&position=top
5. David Moberg, "10 Lessons from the Corporate Collapse," In These Times, August 16, 2002, http://www.inthesetimes.com/issue/26/21/feature2.shtml

6. http://www.inthesetimes.com/issue/26/21/feature2.shtml
7. "Tax Havens: Releasing the hidden billions for poverty eradication," Oxfam Policy Paper, June 2000, http://www.oxfam.org.uk/what_we_do/issues/debt_aid/tax_havens.htm
8. http://www.corpwatch.org/corner/glob/history/
9. http://www.oxfam.org.uk/what_we_do/issues/debt_aid/tax_havens.htm
10. Corporations and Labor, http://www.globalissues.org/TradeRelated/Corporations/Labor.asp#MovingOn
11. http://www.fair.org/media-beat/020711.html
12. http://www.nytimes.com/2002/02/05/opinion/05KRUG.html
13. http://www.oxfam.org.uk/what_we_do/issues/debt_aid/tax_havens.htm
14. http://zmag.org/ZMag/articles/chomrollall.htm
15. http://www.washingtonmonthly.com/features/2000/0007.dorgan.html
16. http://www.corporations.org/welfare/index.html
17. http://www.progress.org/banneker/cw.html
18. http://www.earthisland.org/eijournal/new_articles.cfm?articleID=341&journalID=57
19. http://www.foreignpolicy-infocus.org/papers/cw/index.html
20. http://www.essential.org
21. http://www.alternet.org/issues/index.html?IssueAreaID=30
22. http://www.inthesetimes.com/issue/26/10/feature1_1.shtml
23. http://www.zmag.org/econwatch/econwatch.htm

Conclusion

Just one final appeal to my focus group of people viz. "the swing voters" who decide the fate of the country.

You, the American swing voters, please realize that you have an opportunity right now to change the fate of this great nation like how the British people did in the previous two elections. You must be very careful in making your choice to elect your candidates. To be realistic, you have two sets of evils viz. the democrats and the republicans. As repeatedly said before, I have no regard or respect for any of these evils. But, in view of the existing reality, it is a matter of deciding on the lesser of the two evils. In my opinion, **in the interest of all those homeless, poor, low, middle-income, innocent and helpless group of people**, the choice is obvious for me. My choice is definitely not the republicans. I may not be that bright or well informed like all those republican supporters. **Please give me a factual, not fabricated, account of everything that the republicans have done to uplift the living conditions of the group of people that I mentioned above. Then, I will check it out and vote for the republicans, if the given information happens to be true.** I can't be fairer than this. Can I? Please, don't waste your valuable votes on the independent candidate, as we need a decisive change from top to bottom in all levels of your governments.

Once again, you, the American swing voters, please wake up like how the Spaniards did recently to throw out the right wing government that joined in the unnecessary, illegal and immoral invasion and occupation of Iraq.

It is surprising, sad and shocking to note that still quite a few think that the war on Iraq was well worth it. According to me, these people should fall into one of these two categories.

Warmongers who are true believers and followers of Cheney and Rumsfeld who wanted to invade Iraq ever since Mr. Bush moved to the White House.

The people who are still in the clouds of confusion and refuse to get real and face the facts.

As for the 1st category, there is nothing I can say since they are nothing but an example of real extremists. As for the 2nd category, I would like them to give us the justifying facts for their concept in this context.

How many of their close members of family, friends and relatives were already killed or waiting killing or seriously hurt for life?

Besides the reasons that I provided in the "Working for Living" chapter in this respect, the following are just a few of my additional reasons for this:

• The republicans never ever cared for your welfare. All they cared about is the welfare of the well to do and rich people and massive tax cut to them.
• Don't forget the amount of the taxpayers' money and valuable legislative time they wasted to destabilise and derail the Clintons while they were in the White House. How useful it would have been, if all that money and time were used for all the other pressing issues of the nation at that time?
• Don't forget the ever-increasing number of our own sons, daughters and innocent Iraqi civilians who unnecessarily died already and are facing death in Iraq now.
• Don't forget the ever-increasing national debt created by the republican administration. You, your children and their children have to work ever so hard to pay back this debt.
• Don't forget the recent recommendations made by Greenspan to reduce the national debt. Your social security benefit will be cut since the republicans will religiously take this recommendation as their 11th commandment. Instead of finding every conceivable means to reduce the national debt immediately, they are plotting on to reduce your social security benefit. Just imagine, you worked all these years and made the contributions all along hoping that you can have a decent retired life. Use your head and reasoning.
• Don't forget, your government will continue to be controlled by big corporations and not by your elected representatives.
• Don't forget the influence and impact of campaign contributions.

Republicans will never ever do anything to eliminate this evil influence.

So, please take the ensuing November election as a real crucial decision period of your lifetime. In the interest of your children and their children, do everything possibly you can to ensure the following:

- Every eligible voter makes a careful choice of the candidates and, come what may, does make it a point to vote.
- Every vote counts. Don't forget what happened in Florida election in 2000.

You, the Americans, can send the following strong solid message to the rest of the world by ensuring landslide destruction of the republicans from the power in all local, state and federal levels:

- Enough is enough.
- No more of people's government being controlled by the greedy Corporations.
- People are restoring democracy back and taking control of their government.

In spite of all these appeals to your common sense, if you bring back the republicans to power, then I have nothing to say except to pray to save this great nation from the clutches of the evil vested interests.

Okay, folks, I have been whining and moaning till now hoping that something positive may come out of it. But, honestly to be realistic, I expect the status quo to continue. Nothing positive is likely to happen to uplift the living conditions of the poor, middle and low-income group of people anywhere in the world. Rich will get richer. Poor will continue to stay poor and even may become homeless. In brief, whether we like it or not,

- The concept "government of the people, by the people and for the people" will continue to be a concept only but will not materialize.
- The politicians will continue to be the puppets of the vested interests since the campaign contributions will continue to flow in.
- Corporate greed will continue to grow forever and CEOs will get richer and richer.
- The outsourcing for cheap labour will flourish forever. More corporations

will find tax havens elsewhere. They will pay less tax whereas we will pay more tax.
• Mr. Bush will be back in power again to continue the American global domination.
• More and more bloodshed and mass murders will continue in the Middle East.
• Terrorist activities from both domestic and foreign terrorists will continue.
• Money will always talk and matter everywhere in the world.
• Media propaganda will continue to be in the clutches of the special interests.
• The rich and the chief executives of big corporations will always find ways out to escape from whatever illegal and immoral activities they may do, including the tax evasion.
• Male domination will continue for a very long time.
• **Respecting other races and religions will never happen.**

I sincerely hope and fervently pray that I am proved wrong in what I stated just now. But, my gut feeling is, the status quo will continue. The reason is basic and simple. We are not awake yet and I don't see any indication to the contrary. Until such time we find saviours and leaders like Mahatma Gandhi, Dr. Martin Luther King, Nelson Mandela, etc., we will continue to be in this deep coma and illusion. Most of us are still lazy and lethargic when it comes to any reform. We can use our voting power carefully and effectively to make the democracy work for everyone. But, we won't. We can use peaceful but powerful non-violent methods to put right the injustice being inflicted on ordinary citizens. But, we won't. You know why? Please forgive me for saying this. But, it is a proven fact. Most of us in the "middle of the road category" are still sluggish, stupid and dumb. The extremists, rich, vested interests and the politicians know this very well. Unlike most of us, these people are sharp, smart and shrewd. So, they will continue to screw us forever. They know that we may whine and moan for a few days, but will eventually stop soon.

While I truly believe in our God Almighty, I just wonder what our Almighty is doing when all these atrocities are inflicted on so many innocent people. Besides the never ending violence between the Palestinians and Israelis, **countless** number of innocent Iraqi civilians including women and children will continue to get wiped away from this planet due to unjustified American invasion and occupation.

Is "survival of the fittest" the right answer?

Is "mighty military strength" the right answer?

What happens to the power of prayer for health and happiness for all?

Honestly, I don't know as to how and why these evildoers are able to carry on with their atrocities on the weak and vulnerable. There must be a reason. But, I don't know what it is.

Okay, if I am really convinced that nothing positive is going to happen, then why on earth I wasted my time and your time by stating all those things in various chapters in this book. Let me please explain below.

I was born and brought up in a financially poor background in India. I did child labour to earn some money to buy schoolbooks and luxuries like candies and cookies. However, God blessed me with scholarships and enabled me to educate up to Ph.D. level.

While I was growing up, I have been very critical and concerned of the corruption, bribery, dowry, injustice to innocent people, women and the so-called "untouchables" created by the caste system in India. Besides, having lived in the UK, Saudi Arabia and USA for so long, I did personally witness the exploitation of ordinary citizens by the rich and corrupt politicians. This has been bothering me a lot all the time. But, there is nothing I can do about it except to whine and moan about it.

I'm sure that you know what it is like to keep all your feelings, emotions and grievances pent up within yourself all the time. Even though nothing positive and effective in real terms may happen to you, you feel a bit better, relieved and relaxed when you speak and share your pent up feelings, thoughts and grievances with someone thus unloading whatever that has been bothering you. Hope you understand what I mean. Unfortunately, that "someone" is you, the reader, now and hence this book documenting my thoughts and views.

Besides, I sincerely hope and pray that there may be a remote chance of at least one or two budding born leaders who may happen to read this book, and then hopefully pursue and follow it up further for a positive result to the well being of the humanity. If it ever happens, then, thank God, my effort to share my views and thoughts with every one of you is well worth it and well rewarded.

Let me finish with my fervent prayer to our Almighty to bless everyone, especially those who are unable to help themselves. THANKS for your patience in checking out my thoughts and views. God Bless you all.

About The Author

Perumal Krishnan was born and brought up in India. He had to do child labour to earn some money to buy schoolbooks and luxuries like candies and cookies. However, God blessed him with scholarships for further studies. He has a Master's degree in Engineering. After working for a while in India, he moved to England to work for a Ph.D. degree. On completion of the research, while writing his thesis, he decided to seek employment and settle down in the UK.

In his first job, as an application programmer, he did mathematical modelling and digital simulation of the flight performance of Concorde aircrafts. Then, ever since, he continued his career to develop software for scientific, engineering and commercial applications.

He is living in the USA now with his wife whom he married in 1969. They are blessed with two delightful daughters who continue to live in the UK. The 1st daughter is a Doctor of Medicine working as a paediatrician in London. The 2nd daughter, having earned a M.A. degree in Political Science, is now working as an administrator for a software house.

He lived and worked in various cities in India, England, Saudi Arabia, Germany and the USA. Besides, as tourists along with his family, he had visited various cities in India, the United Kingdom, Europe, Greece, Egypt, Malaysia, Singapore, Thailand, the USA, and Canada. As such, he has been fortunate to meet with people from various parts of the world and witness their varied culture and way of living.

While he was growing up, he had been critical and concerned about the corruption, bribery, dowry, injustice to innocent people, women and the so-called "untouchables" created by the caste system in India. Besides, having lived and worked in India, England, Saudi Arabia and USA for so long, he personally witnessed the exploitation of the ordinary citizens by the corrupt corporations and their puppets viz. the politicians.

He recalls his personal experiences, beliefs and philosophy about life to document in this book his thoughts and views on what is going on with our lives now, and what we can do to be smart and better ourselves. In short, he tries to express his views and thoughts on how to live well and let others also live well at the same time.

Acknowledgments

My deep sense of gratitude goes to the following:

I am deeply indebted to the 1st two groups that enabled me to get this book to you, the readers.

The 1st group consists of all those authors who provided valuable information in their respective websites and books. To the best of my knowledge, I have stated the source from where I collected the supporting data for this book. If, by any chance, I failed to mention any source, I request the authors of those sources to forgive me for my mistake and oversight in this context. This book consists of the collection of all the relevant input data from their contributions to support my views and thoughts on various issues. So, I sincerely THANK each and every one of those authors who enabled me to make this book possible.

The 2nd group consists of all those who made their contribution to publish, market and sell this book everywhere. In particular, I am obliged to the publisher, "PublishAmerica." My heartfelt "THANKS" goes to everyone at this establishment for their professionalism, prompt and positive response at all times. They are a bunch of real good and great professionals. I sincerely hope that they continue to encourage new writers.

I am grateful to my loving and caring wife for her patience while I was deeply engrossed with my research and writing for this book.

Last but not least, it goes without saying, I am indebted to each and every one of you, the readers. THANKS for buying this book and for giving me this opportunity to share my views and thoughts with you all. I repeat my request again. If any of my shared views and suggestions make sense and appear to be acceptable to you, then please act accordingly by doing the right thing at the right time in the right peaceful way, instead of just doing nothing. You should be in-charge to control your own and your country's destiny. Don't leave it in the hands of the dirty politicians. Please DON'T.

Book Order Details

Dear Reader,

It is hoped that this book has been useful, educational and thought provoking to you all giving quite a bit of "Something To Think About."

So, why don't you consider giving this book as a gift to your loved ones, friends, family members and colleagues?

This book is available almost in all the leading bookstores. If you prefer, you can get your copies directly from the publisher following the information provided in these two links:

http://www.publishamerica.com/orderinginfo.htm
http://www.publishamerica.com/shopping/orderform.htm

Thanks again for your participation. It is appreciated.

Printed in the United Kingdom
by Lightning Source UK Ltd.
103866UKS00001B/91